Life Was A Strain
(Gage)

Life Was A Strain (Gage)

From a humble upbringing in the Depression era of West Virginia's coal country to his visionary development of the high-temperature strain gage and pioneering engineering work on jet engines and NASA spacecraft.

P. Allan Hill

This strain gage's wire is one-fourth the diameter of a hair!

Life Was a Strain (Gage) by P. Allan Hill (1928–)

ISBN: 1547275219
ISBN 13: 9781547275212
Edited by Lila Jane (Hill) and Robert C. Morhard
Printed in the United States of America.
Published by ExploConsult, LLC.
Printed by Create Space, an Amazon Company.

Introduction

THIS IS P. Allan Hill's life story from a humble upbringing in the Depression era of West Virginia's coal country and visionary development of the high-temperature strain gage designed and made in his microengineering lab.

P. Allan Hill is my father, and throughout the last thirty-seven years, I have marveled at his microengineering genius. There are many examples where mechanical engineering powerhouses such as NASA, General Electric, Pratt & Whitney Jet Engine Division, Rolls-Royce Jet Engine Division, General Motor's Allison Jet Engine Division, Corning Glass, and many others have come to P. Allan Hill for specialized instrumentation and materials microengineering skills.

P. Allan Hill was the inventor of the world's first semiautomatic strain-gage machine. He has also developed numerous sensors such as thermocouples, accelerometers, and pressure transducers, which are so small that they require a microscope to examine. P. Allan Hill's wire-wound strain gage is incredibly small. The strain gage's wire diameter is amazingly small, 0.8 mil or 0.0008 of an inch or 0.26 the diameter of a human hair, which is 3 mil or 0.003 inch. Allan made thousands of strain gages!

The strain-gage instrumentation, developed by P. Allan Hill, has been an integral part of the many NASA spacecraft and satellites including the Space Shuttle.

P. Allan Hill was the founder of Strain-O-Therm Technology, Inc., and his strain gages have been used for strain testing since the 1970s in the development of the jet-engine turbine fan blades and his strain gages are used by virtually every jet engine manufacturer globally. We can all thank P. Allan Hill, when we look outside the plane at thirty-five thousand feet and know that the jet engine's turbine fan blades tolerate the hostile effects of high-temperature strain and function flawlessly flight after flight.

These are P. Allan Hill's words, all meticulously handwritten with the beautiful handwriting of an old-school mechanical engineer who handmade engineering drawings.

Lila Jane Hill Morhard

Table of Contents

P. Allan Hill's Principles

———— ⁂ ————

"I HAVE WRITTEN my life story so my grandchildren and my great grandchildren will know what my life was like when I was a young boy growing up in the Depression era in the rural mountains of coal country West Virginia."

"After sixty-five years of marriage, Lila Lee Horton has made my life beyond wonderful."

"God is good!"

"Strain gages were always on my mind."

"So many things in life I'll never understand."

"Keep trying and do whatever you do the best that can be done."

"When you do good things, blessings just show up from nowhere and makes your most wonderful life just a whole lot better."

"I felt I could do anything that could be done and all I needed was a chance to try."

"I've got it all. I have been happy with my work and enjoyed my loving family."

"My life has been a blessing from God for sure."

"I have never consumed alcohol."

"I never took a drink, not even a beer while in the navy."

"After thinking about my odd and unusual life I know that I was born to be blessed."

"I felt I could do anything that could be done."

"All I needed was a chance to try."

"I didn't like to lose."

"I'm now eighty-eight and the year is 2017 and I am in near perfect health."

"I sure hope the summer this year will bring good motorcycle weather."

"I am thankful to have born to be blessed."

Apollo Moon Project

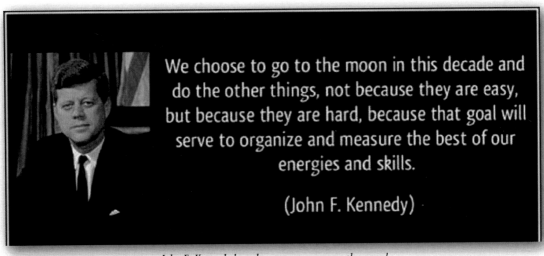

John F. Kennedy has plans to put a man on the moon!

IN 1960, THE rumor at GE's top-secret Aircraft Nuclear Propulsion Department (ANPD) was that the nuclear-powered airplane might be terminated because of nuclear fears by the public. We now had a new US president, John F. Kennedy, and he had other things to do with all this research money. This was 1961, and the ANPD was terminated.

The first experimental flight in the Apollo Moon Project, called at the time the Apollo Man on The Moon Project, was estimated to cost one billion dollars.

GE got the prime contract for the Apollo Moon Project and the project would start in Philadelphia, Pennsylvania. This would require a new facility. It would be called Space Technology Center, located at Valley Forge, Pennsylvania.

The Apollo Moon Project will be at the cutting edge of technology, like the ANPD was ten years before. I'd love to be a part of this new technology, but wanting to won't get me there.

After a few weeks, I started looking to see where I might get other employment. I looked at Procter Gamble Company, and while I was looking, I was asked to stay around a few more days to see what might happen. I was asked if I would like to go to Valley Forge, Pennsylvania, to be a part of the Apollo Moon Project. I knew some of the engineers were asked, but I didn't have any idea I'd be asked. There were two hundred engineers from ANPD who were asked to go. I was working on my PE in engineering but hadn't taken my test yet.

GE asked me to go as an individual contributor on the Apollo Moon Project. And of course I said yes, not even knowing what benefits I'd be getting. I'll no longer be on the clock. The company will pay my moving, pay all expenses on a new home, plus a good increase in pay.

Life can't get any better than this!

I knew this before I even started to work on the Apollo Moon Project!

Life with a lot of different responsibilities wasn't what I wanted. Up until now my responsibilities were limited to projects that I thought need to be worked on. Now life is going to be different: the first thing was I was going to Philadelphia, Pennsylvania, to start my new job. I have got to find a home, and so many things that must be done right now. It was so different than when I started out ten years before. Over the last ten years, I grew into the lifestyle at GE and the Cincinnati area. Now I'm dumped into a much different lifestyle. I thought I'll have to learn to adjust to a new lifestyle, which I did, but it took a few months.

Making the move to the Apollo Moon Project will be a great part of my life in the next ten years.

When I was transferred to Philadelphia, Pennsylvania, to work at the GE Space Technology Center, there were no GE operations at Valley Forge, Pennsylvania. The construction was started, but in the meantime, I worked at a GE facility in downtown Philadelphia on the 32nd and Chestnut Streets, while the GE Space Technology Center was being built in Valley Forge thirty-eight miles from downtown. I worked at the downtown lab for approximately two years; sometimes GE would bus some of us to Valley Forge to make sure our facility was OK.

When I started working at the GE Space Technology Center at Valley Forge, I bought a home close as I could to Valley Forge, Pennsylvania, because that was where I'd be working as soon as the center was built. Most of the employees who would be working at GE wanted a good school for their children. This made homes hard to find. I found a home being built that was much bigger than our home in Cincinnati, Ohio. The price was $16,500. Note: the same home was sold in 2010 for $337,000. We lived in it for ten years, and I don't remember what we sold it for, but I'm sure it was not a windfall for me.

There were several GE employees in the neighborhood, and we at first had to get to work downtown. We formed a car pool. We drove to a bus station approximately five miles and then took a bus over to the subway station. Most of the engineers who came from the ANPD program in Cincinnati, Ohio, started being assigned to other parts of the Apollo Moon Project program.

I had a good friend, Fred Wells, who worked with me, although I worked for him back in the ANPD project. Two months after starting at the Apollo Moon Project, Fred bought a home. After two weeks, he moved his family from Cincinnati, Ohio, into their new home. Fred was sent to the Cape in Florida. He was there for two or three months and was sent to a base in Mississippi. Then for a few months, he was sent back to the Cape. Then to Red Stone Arsenal in Huntsville, Alabama, when that was the last time I heard of him. Fred Wells was one of the engineers who helped me along the way. I didn't know many employees who were transferred from the ANPD project who stayed where they were first assigned. I stayed for ten years and lived through the hard times of setting up production.

Each part of the Apollo space vehicle had to be tested. Now this was after the production got started. The first year and a half for me was at the facility at 32nd and Chestnut Streets, Philadelphia, planning for what we would do at the Space Technology Center being built at Valley Forge. Valley Forge was thirty-eight miles from 32nd Street. After the center was started, I'd get to ride a GE bus to Valley Forge to help plan a future testing lab. After all my friends had been moved from one location to another, I was worried I'd be moved someday.

The life at the Apollo project wasn't yet my liking, not like how I loved my work at ANPD, in Cincinnati, Ohio.

My first thought to ask Dr. Ayers was about my friend Fred Well. I lost track of him when he went back to work at Red Stone Arsenal. Dr. Ayers is the Red Stone Arsenal project manager, so I wasn't sure he would know Fred. He did give me a good report on his work there. Fred left the work at Red Stone and went into radio talk. He died while working on the radio-talk program. I can understand why Dr. Ayer knew Fred because I'm sure Fred was a great employee.

After the GE Space Technology Center was finished, my work started. Up until then, my time was spent in planning, and now it was the actual work. Our first project was going to require a weather spacecraft for the Apollo project. The weather spacecraft was called NIMBUS. There will be a lot of testing for each part. Each part had to be tested to make sure it works with all the other parts. My job was to work with electrical and mechanical systems. I was called the systems test conductor. My first job was to find someone to be assistant, someone I knew that I could depend on. My first thought was a friend back at ANPD, Bryce Kennedy. Now Bryce could do anything, and I needed someone just like Bryce, but there was problem with the salary. Bryce and I had worked together at ANPD. Bryce started out with the ANPD project in Oak Ridge Atomic Energy Group in 1950, and then the project was moved to the Jet Engine Department in Cincinnati, Ohio, in 1954 when I started. Bryce was a pay grade 14. I came to know that there were only two employees at GE with that pay grade. I was a 13, so when there were two hundred of the employees from the ANPD transferred to the space project, Apollo, I was one of them. But my title was Individual Contributor, and I was now off the clock and in management. So, to get Bryce to help me, we had to get the salary worked out. The best I could do was get him to work for me at pay grade 12, which meant a big pay cut. I couldn't get Bryce any help moving and some of the benefits I got, but he wanted to be a part of this Apollo project. So, Bryce became my first employee.

We worked on this NIMBUS weather spacecraft for over a year. Everything that could go wrong went wrong with the testing of the spacecraft, and this was after a year working behind schedule. My boss came to me and asked, not demanded, if I'd work twelve hours a day for six days a week for a year. This was without overtime except Saturday. I wouldn't get paid on Saturday if I missed working overtime one of the week days. What could I say? By the way, he more than made it up to me a year later. While I was working all these hours, Bryce was working too. He worked overtime on some Sundays. He was always telling me, "I'm making more money than you." Of course, he was, but he didn't know what my salary was.

I worked on the NIMBUS weather craft for over sixteen months. This being something new, there was problem after problem. I had responsibility like I'd never had before, and I was working long hours. GE had a room at the local motel where we could go get a few minutes' rest, which I never took advantage of. I just kept working.

The NIMBUS weather satellite was now ready to be tested as a complete vehicle. It was placed on a large vibration table, which would shake the vehicle at the vibration it would get at the top of the missile being sent into space. You wouldn't believe how much the vehicle shook while being tested.

P. Allan Hill worked on the NIMBUS weather satellite.

One of the major tests was to test the solar panels. There were two solar panels about the size of a regular house door. The panels were folded around the craft. So, the spacecraft, known then as a space vehicle, will fit into a container, which is on top of the rocket motor. Once the vehicle is in space, the container ejects the space vehicle, and it was now in free flight in space. This happens after an explosive is activated and the solar panels deploy or unfold so that they are aligned with the sun.

While the space vehicle was on the shaker table or vibration table, the panels were locked in place with a small bolt, which was cut with an explosive when it gets into outer space. This test was to see if everything will work after all this vibration. Now this vehicle was over a year behind NASA's schedule to be tested so this was a very important test.

There were several NASA people along with Mr. Page, vice president of GE, to watch this test. Everything was going fine; I had now been at the vehicle over thirty hours without any sleep. I was excited when the shaking was over and the explosive was set off to see if everything worked OK. It didn't. I forgot that I had placed a temporary pin in place so that if someone made a mistake and set the explosive off, the panels wouldn't unfold. I was so tired that I forgot to remove the temporary pin before testing. This was a big disappointment to Mr. Page and he told me so. I was tired and wanted to go home, but Mr. Page demanded to know where do we go from here. I was in the hot seat and had to deliver.

The space vehicle must be taken off the shaker table to make some repairs. There was some insulation at the very top of the vehicle that must be replaced. My estimate of the time was five days to remove the vehicle from the shaker table, a few minutes to replace the insulation, and five or six days to make the vehicle ready to test again. Mr. Page said he wanted me to prepare a written procedure for each step of getting the vehicle ready for test, and he wanted this information soon. He wasn't a happy man.

I wanted to go home, but I wanted to think this problem over and study how to solve this complex problem. I could see the only problem was the insulation that had to be replaced at the top of the thirty-foot vehicle. It's way up there, but if someone would lift me up with a hoist, and lower me down to the vehicle top with the insulation, I can remove the old insulation and replace it in a few minutes. The crew made me a chair that I could sit on while I was doing the repair, and I was confident I could fix things without any problem. I told the crew, "I'm going home to get some rest and I'll be back soon, but don't start removing the vehicle." I went home to sleep for a few minutes and Hutchie told me Mr. Page was on the phone. He started talking, and for maybe a minute, I didn't know who I was, where I was, or who I was talking to. It was a feeling I'd never had or had since, but I requested him that I will come in and explain why I disobeyed his orders. I left soon as I hung up the phone. The crew got the insulation while I was home, and all I had to do was show Mr. Page my idea when I replaced it while he watched.

No one I've ever known would disobey the vice president of GE like I did, but when you're as tired as I was, you don't think correctly, don't know what you are thinking, and you only wanted to go sleep.

The vibration test was used for many parts of the vehicle. One test that also interested me was the Bulova watches. A timepiece had to be accurate; I think it was two seconds a year. This timepiece would turn on a component a year later. There were five Bulova Accutron watches tested to see how they would hold up under the vibration. Only one passed the test and it just did. This caused a lot of conversation about what better timepiece can we find. Of course, Bulova Accutron is by far the best over time. I was never a lover of Accutron watches. If you're working in an office where you don't have a lot of vibration, then this watch is OK, but this watch is not good if you're running a jack hammer. This watch can't take the force on a small spring that is the heart of the movement. I spent all the time I could with the Bulova engineers, because my background is in horology or watch making. Anyway, I was told NASA had clearly told the engineers that something had to be developed that would be accurate while being vibrated on the rocket during the launch sequence.

After the test was completed, I never heard from Mr. Page, but I got some good news from NASA for all the time I saved by not removing the space vehicle from the shaker table. My last job on NIMBUS was when I went to Oklahoma City, Oklahoma, to check out the canister that the NIMBUS would put in when the satellite went into space. There was another job I was assigned to. I never heard anything about the future of the NIMBUS.

A Young Boy with a Dream

THIS IS A story of a young boy with a dream. What makes this story different is my life has been so much different than the average young boy. I was born in Bud, West Virginia, in Wyoming County on July 9, 1928. This was an old small coal town. The coal company owned the small homes. Our home was one of the most desired than most because there was a water hand pump just out our gate.

We moved from this house when I was maybe six months old to Princeton, West Virginia. While living there, the house burned down. Dad moved back to the house where I was born. We lived there for nearly six months when the 1929 Depression hit the country. Dad got a job as a black-smith helper at a railroad car shop. That job was short-lived because of the Depression; now Dad didn't have money to pay rent. One of the reasons I think my life is different is because of Dad's temper, his state of mind. He had a chip on his shoulder and was never happy about life. Looking back, I think I can now understand his problem. As a young man, Dad got into the trucking business with one of his brothers. He had two large trucks, a Reo and large Chevrolet. He had bought a house in Princeton, West Virginia, that had burned down, and now the world had fallen in on him. He lost his trucks, had no job, and in a Depression. You can understand how bad you can feel, but Dad seemed to try to make everyone around him unhappy too. Now it was when Dad took a job as a blacksmith helper at the railroad and it didn't last long. It seemed everyone was out of work. Dad spent much of his time looking for any work just for food and rent. Without a car, Dad, as many men, would hop a freight train "Hobo" to another town to do everything to make a dollar. While on a boxcar (hoboing) home, he found a large beautiful suitcase full of lots of things, some gold money, a Santa Claus made of celluloid, which I got for Christmas, my first toy. There were some letters, which mother and Dad thought they were code of some kind. I was too young to remember; I just remember Dad was afraid to cash the gold. I think Dad said it was something like twenty dollars. Mother said my Christmas present was an orange and the Santa Claus that year. Dad couldn't find a job, so without rent he had to move from the coal company house. We moved to a rundown house with dirty floors. It was about three miles from mother's folks, which was about three miles from anyone else.

Mother's family were self-supporting people. They lived on what they made by hand—livestock for food, sheep for wool and food, the wood, which they sold for money to buy sugar and things they can't make. Honeybees made some of the honey, which was an everyday food. I enjoyed my visits to Grandma Ball; their home was a log home, one room with a big fireplace. There was a room added to the log home, which was used as a kitchen. There was an upstairs bedroom. You had to go outside to walk up a set of stairs to get there. To grandma the Depression didn't create a lot of problems because she didn't depend on the outside world for much anyway. We lived at that rundown house for a few months, and Dad got a part-time job at the coalmines in Bud, West Virginia. We got a larger home this time. Dad was now working as a blacksmith at the mines. Mother had a lot to do now. I had a sister, and I was about three, so mother had lots of washing to do. She had a day to wash clothes, a day to iron. Since her washing was in a washtub, the tub sat on top of a fire out in the yard, and she did her washing on a washboard. She had to carry the water for washing and had to build her fire to heat her wash water. I'll never forget something that happened one day. I was about three years old when a rainstorm started. Mother's fire was still burning when it started to rain. There were frogs about the size of a dime. It was like a hailstorm. There were thousands of small frogs on the ground. I got some frogs, put them in a pan, and put the pan on the fire. Mother came out and asked what I was doing; I said I was cooking frogs. Most people I tell this to said it didn't happen, but I know it did.

I don't remember much about my life at three or four years old, but one thing I do remember while we lived was there was a death in the family across the road from our house. Everyone was very excited and crying, and I didn't understand. Later mother told me what happened. The father of the family liked to drink his moonshine. He kept the bottle in a shed at the back, and he found someone had been drinking some of it. So, he thought, "I'll fix that problem." He ground up some glass and put it in the moonshine bottle. His fifteen-year-old son drank it and died. We lived there for one or two years. Dad always had ideas; sometimes I think it was something to make mother work harder. Anyway, whatever Dad's ideas were, we had to agree. Mother never had anything to say about what Dad wanted to do. This move was to a mountaintop, a house that belonged to a land company. It was a lease, which cost ten dollars per year. This house was another rundown old house, about three miles from his work. Dad traded a cow for a 1926 Chevrolet convertible four-door car. Dad used the car to drive to work and haul hay from the field. You couldn't get the car all the way to our house, so Dad had to walk a quarter mile from where the car would stop. This lease was called Bear Waller Mountain, because it was where the bears came to play. I never did see one there. I was three or four years old then. Dad would cut wood so that mother could build a fire to do her washing. I had to carry the wood from the forest. Dad sometimes would carry lumps of coal from work so we would have heat in the house. Mother always required wood for her cook stove. Dad always thought ahead what he planned to do. No man I've ever known was half the man Dad was. He was strong, he wanted to work two or three extra jobs, and he was the best at all of them.

We lived on this mountaintop for two or three years. Sometimes he wouldn't come home for a few days. He wouldn't come home the whole weekend sometimes. He didn't work at the mines every day, but if he wasn't in the field on a day off, he stayed down at the coal camp. He had bought a small plot of land to build a home and was getting materials and everything required for building a nice home. This was a piece of private property across the creek from the coal company homes. There were approximately twelve homes on private land. While living on Bear Waller, a man was hunting and a tree fell across the path, and he needed an ax to clear the road. He asked mother for an ax, and she sent me to get the ax for him. He paid me ten cents; I thought I was rich. I used those ten cents a year buying candy corn. I'd buy one cent each time I got to a store. The day came to move back to civilization. I was about five or six years old. I was completely happy living in the woods. Some of the things I recall are when the sun would go down, mother would get a small jar with a rag soaked with kerosene to make a smoke to keep the bugs away while we sat on the porch listening to the whip-poor-wills at night. It didn't take long to find friends to play with. Dad was home all the time now, and he thought I was old enough to be responsible for some duties around the house. In fact, after a year Dad had a garden, a cow, pigs, chickens, and I got to work.

We had electric power but no water. Our good neighbor let us get water from their well. We now had a refrigerator; now we were living first class. Our neighbor next door was Jim Basconnie from Italy. Jim had a brother, Domeneck, and another, Pete, who had a gas station. Jim had a store for food. Domeneck, had a hardware store and feed for livestock. Gas was eleven cents per gallon. This was the only gas station for five miles. The one pump had a handle pump where you pumped the amount of gas you wanted into a glass tube at the top of the pump. The tube had lines showing how many gallons you had to pay for. I don't know anyone who owned a car. Dad left the 1926 Chevrolet at Bear Waller Mountain. It wasn't worth moving.

The Depression was on and it was 1933. We were now settled where we had neighbors. There was a school where I could make friends. Most of my friends were from the coal camp across the creek. Dad was working full time now. His work was at the mines' blacksmith shop. Dad worked from daylight till dark, every day except Sunday. Sometimes he worked on Sundays too. One thing for sure, we never went hungry. We had the same thing to eat mostly every day. Breakfast was biscuits with gravy; dinner was a glass of buttermilk with a piece of corn bread mixed together. Supper was the same every day—cornbread and soup beans. Some Sundays we would have chicken and dumplings. We had a few chickens; mother wouldn't kill a young chicken that was laying eggs. So, when a chicken stopped laying eggs, I'd have the job of killing the old hen. I'd take the hen out to the wood chop block, cut its head off, and then it was mother's job from here. Mother said old chickens are good for chicken and dumplings, not frying. So, I never ate a piece of fried chicken unless it was at a church dinner. I loved the chicken and dumplings best anyway.

At the age of five or six, mother and Dad found lots of work for me. Gathering eggs, feeding the chickens, slopping the pigs, hunting the cow. Cows ran wild back then. I always knew our cow because it had a bell, which I would recognize so I would know where to look. Mother and Dad came from families that knew how to work. Mother would sell eggs, which I had to deliver for six cents per dozen. I had to churn to make butter, from buttermilk, which I had to deliver. Mother got an idea for me. She got a magazine with a sample of mottos. Things like "God Bless This Home" mottos cost me twenty-five cents and I sold them for seventy-five cents. I'd take the samples around the homes in the coal camp and take orders. Then I'd order the motto and deliver them. I made four dollars at that. My dream was to buy a bicycle, but Dad and mother thought I needed a big wagon. They wanted me to go around the neighborhood and pick up the cow manure, which was dried from the sun. It was what Dad used as the fertilizer for the garden. Dad always thought of work, not play. The first week I had my wagon, Dad got the idea of getting some coal for our heating. There was an old coal mine not far away. Dad got some tools and a carbide light, which was the only light you could carry at that time. At least the only one I knew about. I'd hold the light while Dad would dig the coal, which he would load into my wagon and he also had a wheelbarrow. Dad would never pay for anything free. This was a very dangerous thing to do; the top could fall in anytime. I got some five-gallon buckets, put them in the wagon, and would go around the neighborhood coal camp and pick up the leftover food from the supper meal. This is what I'd take home and feed the pigs. I called it slopping the hogs. At Thanksgiving time it was a very busy time for killing the hogs. I think the coal camp had a Butcher Hollow where the hogs were taken to be slaughtered. Very few people had cooling to keep the meat. Thanksgiving was in cooler weather and seemed the right time for slaughtering. I could only haul a hog, which was dead in my wagon. I watched many being killed, and everyone had their idea how best to kill the hog. Dad seemed to master how to do everything better than anyone else. Dad would hit the hog between the eyes, the hog would fall stunned, and Dad would cut its throat; all the bleeding was done before it got to Butcher's Hollow. I've seen so many people shoot the hog and it didn't kill it. It's hard to get another shot, as the hog goes wild. Lots of the men would ask Dad to kill the hogs for them because Dad made it look so easy. My big wagon was just what was needed for taking the hogs to Butcher Hollow.

Sometimes I'd make maybe seven dollars at Thanksgiving time. There was a lot of slaughtering taking place that day and weekend. Back then five cents was about equal to five dollars today. I never did like to be around when the slaughtering took place, but it was a part of life. I sure do remember the smell of the sausage when mother made it fresh. Mother was good at making something to eat out of every piece of meat. Most of the meat was canned and put away for another day, and even the brains were used for food. This slaughtering at Thanksgiving time was a very big time of the year, at Butcher Hollow. My wagon did get a workout that weekend and made it worth more than you would ever know, because that was only the beginning of its worth.

Dad was the company's blacksmith; there were several families from Italy who worked with stone cutting. When these men needed to sharpen their tools, they would come to Dad who would rework their tools so they could go back to work. Dad got an idea—there was old steel material here at the mine, using which he could make his own tools. Now if they can cut stone, he can too. Dad found some stone in a small creek about a mile from our home. Dad wasn't the average man. He had to be the best at anything he would do. So after working at the mines as a blacksmith, he would go directly to cutting stone until dark. Now to get his tools was my job. I'd load his tools up in my wagon; his dinner and I'd have to be where he was cutting stone when he got there. A note about my education. While other kids were getting schoolwork, I never had the chance to study.

Dad's always told me, "If you are a coal miner, boy, then school is not important."

The only thing you need to know is how to work hard and always be honest.

When I'd take the tools to Dad, I'd have to help him just like a man. I'd have to remove dirt from on top of some stone. Dad asked me to cut stone, which hadn't been cooked by the sun. Sometimes we might be driving somewhere after we got a truck. Dad would see a stone in a field, and he'd stop, go cut the stone to see if he liked it or not. He had to be a master at everything he did.

This part of the story was forty years later. He had a stone wall to build when he was seventy-two years old. He put up the most beautiful wall I've ever seen. People would say to him what a wonderful mason you are and Dad would comment, "I'm not a stone mason, but I'm a blacksmith." Now Dad had cut stone, and he needed a truck to haul the stone. He bought a 1934 Ford, a big truck, which had been used for the logging business. Even if it wasn't old it was worn out.

Dad wasn't happy if he couldn't find something for me to do. There were always things to do. Feed the pigs, feed the chickens, go cow hunting. One time the cow went into a new area. I could hear her cowbell. So I went in that direction. I got deeper into the woods, and dogs started barking at me. About this time two men came to me and asked why I was there. There was moonshine still up there, and they had dogs as their guards. I got my cow and went home. Milking time was a time I hated. Mother said I let my fingernails grow long just to make the cow uncomfortable while I was milking. A few times the cow kicked the milk bucket over while I was milking. With stone cutting, cow hunting, and feeding the hogs, Dad found another job for me. With this big truck, he could see a use for it where he could make an extra dollar. There was a sawmill close by; they had a big supply of slabs. A slab is a piece of the log you cut first. It wasn't any good for lumber; it was a by-product, which had to be hauled away. Dad could see where he could make a dollar. Dad hauled all he could on the truck for one dollar, and he would take the load home, cut it into one-foot lengths for firewood, and sell them for five dollars. Dad would take the truck to the sawmill on the way to work. He would park the truck where I could start loading the slabs as soon as school was over. He would come after work at the mine and then we would deliver the load and go home. Just another way Dad had for making a dollar.

This was a time I was about six years old. I could see that friends from school saw me different. Dad's projects kept me busy.

Dad and mother never had a conversation that wasn't yelling or fighting about something. I thought mother was a little crazy, but I guess it was because of the way Dad treated her. Dad was a lot crazy, but a lot mean. It seemed Dad was making a new problem for the family almost every day now. One night he went to the church meeting, and put a burlap sack over his head and yelled, "I'm the devil." The police came and took him to jail. I felt so embarrassed and ashamed of some of the things Dad did. When your friends at school said you're the son of the devil. At this part of my life, it seemed Dad made trouble all the time. Dad and mother fought all the time. Mother would lock Dad out, and he'd knock the door down. He'd get his pistol out and say, "I'll just kill all of us and solve this problem." The police would take him off to jail again.

I don't know why I was never afraid of Dad. But my sister who was two years younger than me cried all the time. At a time when all this was going on, one weekend Dad decided to go visit Grandma Hill in Princeton, West Virginia. The only transportation we had was this old truck. To get there you must go over a steep mountain. The old truck engine overheated, and Dad had to stop on the mountain. I was sitting on the truck bed, mother was holding my sister, and my young brother was just a baby. Dad and mother went yelling again. I heard everything they said because the back glass was broken. While the truck was stopped, Dad said, "I'll just back the truck over the mountain and kill all of us." As the truck started to drift back, I was afraid for the first time. Of course he didn't, but the wheels were so close to the edge before he stopped.

Another time I was ashamed was the only other boy I had as a friend found out what Dad was like. Dad had removed some railroad ties from the coal camp and put them in a pile, so he could come back with his truck to get them. When he came back, some of the ties were gone. Dad thought he knew who got them. So, he went home, got his pistol, went to the man, and demanded to return the ties. Of course, he returned the ties, but this ended the friendship of my only friend I had at that time. It was his father who had removed the ties.

Everything I can remember was different from anyone my age at that time. Sometimes I think how Dad was. He wasn't a good father, but he taught me things no other father could teach a child. He was to me a great genius at everything he attempted to do. The things Dad taught me you don't find in a book. Sometimes I think Dad's thoughts about just learn to work hard and work smart, and be honest is all you do, is all you need to know to get by. Dad made a wooden box for all his stone-cutting tools that I could put in my wagon and take to his work where he was cutting stone. I was learning things that would be important to me later in life that were not found in school.

Dad's work wasn't just work; he would study a stone like a great diamond cutter. Dad had a name for me; I thought it must be my name as I heard it so much. He said you're a dumb stupid idiot and you'll never amount to anything. Maybe that would hurt some kids, but it only made me try harder to satisfy my Dad. Dad got a contract to work in the town of Mullens, West Virginia.

This was June 1935. School was out. I was seven years old. I'd be eight years in July. Mother packed my lunch and I walked to Mullens, which was five miles away. One thing I remember about that job was while walking along the road, I was asked to pick up old cigarettes, take the tobacco out, and put it in a little sack my friend had given me. He couldn't afford five cents a pack for cigarettes. When I got to work, Dad called my job "keeping time."

There were three men working for Dad on this job. Dad was working at the mine. Now Dad didn't want anyone sitting around, so you had to stay busy. So, I kept busy all day till Dad got off work at the mine and he would come and get me to go home. I worked at that job all summer. With all the work I had to do, there was always time to have some fun. At eight years, I had a few friends, and we found something to do every weekend. We would go to the woods, find a grapevine, and swing. We started trying to see how long we could stay off the ground by swinging from tree to tree. We would swing from one tree limb to another, seeing who could stay off the ground the longest. None of my friends were overweight.

Kids Should Not Play on Coal Mine Slate Dumps

---- ✎ ----

ONE GREAT STORY in my early years when I was approximately eight years old and one of the reasons I'm "born to be blessed" was because at an early age the Lord saved me from a very stupid thing I did with two of my friends. There was a small railroad called tram road where the coal was hauled from the mine to where it was loaded into railroad cars. When the coal was brought out of the mine in a mine car, it was dumped into a tipple where the coal was placed on a conveyor, going to be loaded into the railroad car. As the conveyor moved along, there were several men picking out stone, which didn't belong in the railroad car. They were called "bone pickers." That was my first job at the mine. This stone, or what we called bone, went into another conveyor, which went into a large truck, or into another mine car, and was taken to a slate dump. It was a product that was worthless, and over many years it became a mountain that we called the slate dump. There was a slab pile nearly one hundred years old, which started up in the mountain and was very steep. And over the years it was maybe four hundred or five hundred feet long down the mountain.

Bill Lester who was eight years old, his brother, Buzz Lester, who was six years old, and I thought we would have some fun at the slate dump. Remember, every kid at the coal camp was told never to go to the slate dump. We found a sheet of tin three feet wide, ten feet long. We bent the front of the sheet like a bobsled. Buzz got on first while Bill was holding the sled. I got on behind Buzz, put my legs around him, and the sled took off leaving Bill alone. Bill rolled down the slate dump a few feet while Buzz and I were moving on. The best I can remember was we were "in the air" more than once on the slate dump. After going down the dump a few feet, I remembered there was a barbed wire fence across the bottom of the dump. I tried to get off, but I couldn't get my legs from around Buzz. We are going so fast that there wasn't anything I could do. As our luck would have it, some many years ago a large tree had fallen across the slate dump. At this part of the slate dump, it was about thirty or forty feet wide. The slate had washed to the tree, which had fallen. The tree was about twenty feet from the end of the dump and the barbed wire fence. We shot over the fence a few feet and into a tree. It was spring time and it had lots of new foliage. Buzz, being in front, took the shock of my body. Buzz had several compound fractures and his bones were sticking out of his clothes. He couldn't get up and walk so Bill had to stay with him while I went to get help. I ended up with a broken nose, shoulder, and jaw, and my nose was hurt. I had to walk approximately a quarter mile to get help. On the way, my nose was bleeding so I stopped to wash the blood away in the creek water. That was a big mistake because all homes had their toilets empty into the creek. I almost died from blood poison because of the filth in the water, at the creek. Dr. Lester wrote about Buzz's accident in his book. God was with us that day. Looking back even now, a two-year-old would have known better.

At eight I loved to fish when I had time off. There was a log dam on Barkers Creek, which was there before railroads and car roads. The timber business in West Virginia was the main business. Lumber companies would find a good place to build a dam, where mountains were steep and the creek was narrow. They would build a strong dam of stone, maybe thirty or forty inches thick. In the center of the dam, there was an opening space approximately forty inches wide made of logs and sealed with clay to make a temporary dam. The dam would fill up with water, with thousands of logs that had been cut washed down to where a train was waiting to load the logs and take them to a sawmill. When the dam was full of logs, they would use dynamite to blast a forty-inch wide hole in the temporary part of the dam and the logs would wash down to Mullens, West Virginia, to be loaded on to the train railcars, which took them to the sawmill. After approximately seventy or a hundred years later, what was left of this dam is a great fishing hole. I was told to stay away from the old dam. One day I saw there was a big log, part of the dam left in the dam, which was sticking out over the dam, and I thought I could sit on it and fish.

I was seven or eight at the time. I guess I forgot about the time, so here comes mom, and she wasn't happy. She whipped me every step of the way home. The reason she was so unhappy was because I had a chore to be done before Dad got home. I had to have the bean bugs picked off the beans before Dad got home from work. My job was to get a small jar, put some kerosene in it, pick the bugs off the beans, and put the bugs in the jar where they died. I sure did love fishing. I'd get a straight pin, bend it like a hook, get some sewing thread from mother, get a limb from a small tree, and go fishing. I don't remember catching anything big. With this hook the fish got away, but I loved trying to catch a fish. There was a project some men in the coal camp started. I don't know if it was a West Virginia state or coal company project. It was something to keep the boys active. If you killed a snake you got points: a black snake would get you some points and a rattler or copperhead gave so many points. You got points for an English sparrow right wing. If you got so many points, you got a gift. I don't remember getting anything, but I spent a lot of Sundays looking. I got so good with a slingshot that I would kill whatever I tried to hit. A friend and I went squirrel hunting, walking on the tram road, and we saw a squirrel on a tree. We used our slingshots and killed the squirrel. I don't know which one of us did it, but it made both of us happy, because we sure were good with a slingshot.

Lila Lee Horton (a.k.a. "Hutchie")

LIFE IN OUR house, not a home, was pure hell. Dad and mother fought every day. Dad was a very demanding person. Dad and mother would fight and mother would lock the door, Dad would break the door down, and the police would come and take Dad away to jail. In all this my only problem was what people thought and how ashamed I was of my mother and Dad. But I always thought Dad caused all the problems. At a young age, you learn to live with it, but I always had a desire to be happy someday. I had no idea what love was about. I took a cute little girl back to her home after our first date. When I met her family, I was in a state of shock to see how the Horton family seemed to enjoy life. I had never seen anyone at home smile about anything.

Lila Lee Horton (my "Hutchie") aged fifteen.

My first girlfriend was Lila Horton and was someone whom I'd never seen before. On our first date, she was fifteen years old and I was eighteen, just out of the navy. We ended up in her house; I can't explain what I thought about that family. They laughed; they acted like everyone loved each other. I told my sweetheart I fell in love with her family before I did with her. Lila and I had many more dates after that, and I was pleasantly surprised that she agreed to marry me.

My wife Hutchie did all the things at home that I should be doing. I look back and can't believe what I put her through. She never complained.

I believe our love affair has been the best and maybe the longest. It's now been sixty-five years, and I hope there is a lot more to come.

After sixty-five years, Lila has made my life beyond wonderful. God is good!

I Am the Oldest of Seven Children

———— ✿ ————

I'M THE OLDEST of the seven children in our family. I have one brother twelve years younger than me. He is married to a wonderful woman and has a wonderful family. The other brothers and sisters haven't been as fortunate as we were. Dad and mother got a divorce when my two younger sisters were fifteen and thirteen years old. Dad and mother moved out and left all of us without a home.

I now have a wonderful job with the General Electric Company.

With the help of my brother, David, we did our best to make life livable for our sisters. I asked myself why am I so blessed? Why can't everyone be as happy as I am? I'm the oldest of the seven, and David is twelve years younger than me. Now, in 2017, only my brother, David, and I are still alive.

Cigarettes and whiskey have caused a lot of problems.

I'm proud to say I've never had a beer in my life.

I've got too much to be happy for, and all I need is a loving home. God is good. David and I meet for breakfast often.

Dad always told me that education isn't important, but just learn to work hard and you'll get by.

It was 1939 and the war was on everyone's mind. I was eleven years old and spent a lot of time with my wagon, gathering anything that could be used for the war effort. The mines now were working full-time. Dad had built a wonderful house, but it wasn't a home. Mr. and Mrs. Church lived across the street. Mr. Church told Dad he had some property that he would like to trade with Dad for our house. They had a timber business about thirty miles in the mountains.

Dad said we need a few acres so we can grow things to eat after the war starts. Looking back, I think Dad could see this war was a way for him to get away from the family. Dad made the deal. He would work full time at the mine, stay at the mine, come home Friday, and go back to work Sunday evening. This property trading took place in perhaps 1940. The area where we moved was Basin, West Virginia. Very few people ever heard of Basin. It was eight miles from Rt. 16, Stephenson, West Virginia, and eight miles West from Herndon, West Virginia, Rt. 10. It had no electric power and not much of anything but thirty-six acres. It was new and no one had lived in that place for four or five years.

Basin, West Virginia: 1939—1943

—— ❧ ——

THIS NEW HOME, a house wasn't what you would call, even back then was a good place to live. Dad didn't know all the problems he had made for his family. Dad stayed at the coal mine and would only come home on the weekends. Dad bought a new truck, a 1940 Chevrolet pickup. I remember how proud I was, but Dad thought it cost too much. It was new and cost $740.

As a ten-year-old, there was so much to do, and it was all new for me. I had to take responsibility of all the chores, which were many. The house was approximately one thousand square feet. It had a large kitchen, with room for the cook stove, which was set at the corner of the kitchen. At the space behind the stove was a large wash tub, which we used for our bath. The cook stove had a water tank as part of the stove so we had warm water for the bath. There was a large wood box besides the stove for mother's cooking. This room was for cooking and eating. Another room was for sitting, and in it we had a small pot belly stove, which used coal for heat. There were two bed rooms. The house was new, although it was about four years old. The siding boards had warped or seasoned and you could pass your fingers through the cracks. Mother got a newspaper from the friend she knew at the coal camp. Dad would bring newspapers home on the weekend. Mother would make a paste from cooking flour and water, soak the newspaper with paste, and plaster it on the inside of the wall.

My job was milking the cow and cutting wood for the stove. I learned that you want good dry kindling to start a fire. It was my job to have the cook stove hot when mother started breakfast. Also, when it was zero degrees outside, it was zero degrees inside, so you got a fire going fast in the pot belly stove. I used coal often to start the fire, and if I had enough slack coal, I could also set the air dampeners on the stove so the fire would burn all night. While looking for a good kindling, thoughts went back to when I was about four or five years old. Dad took me up a hill when there was a big chestnut tree. Dad had a large bag full of these wonderful chestnuts. Then around 1931 or 1932, we went back and the chestnut tree had died. No more chestnut trees, so when I went to get kindling, I'd find a chestnut tree that had died.

There wasn't any electric power in Basin, West Virginia. We did have running water, if you call it that. Dad had dammed up a small stream of water, which was piped into our kitchen. Now the cook stove was mother's pride. No coal would ever go in mother's stove, only good solid dry wood. Mother had to have the fire just right for cooking. We had a breakfast of biscuits and gravy every morning. A typical breakfast was biscuits and gravy, buttermilk with cornbread, and for supper it was cornbread and soup beans. Of course, we had lots of other things to eat. Mother canned all the food we could find in the summer.

The only things we had to buy were sugar, flour, and lamp oil. We bought the flour in twenty-five-pound bags, and mother used a lot of them. We used a lot of meal for corn bread. Under our house was a cellar where we kept canned goods and other foods. We had five wooden barrels, each five gallons, loaded with pickled beans, one of cut up cabbage, called kraut. One with cucumbers and one with pickled beets, and one with maybe two or three hundred cobs of corn. There were large rocks on top of the corn to keep them down into the brine. I've got many ears of corn out of the barrel when no one knew about it. It was cold, but good. Mother canned all our food, and anything she could, and it was so good.

We killed the cow once when it wasn't producing milk. Mother canned the meat. Most of all I liked the different ways mother could can the berries. We had pigs at first. Dad thought he would raise pigs, take them to the coal camp, and sell them. Our first litter had eight little pigs, and all of them were blind. I don't remember what Dad did with them; I just remember he give up on raising pigs. It was very difficult doing many things with no electric power.

When we ran out of meal, I'd take a sack of corn up to Mr. McKinney's mill. They lived approximately a quarter mile up the creek from our home. Basin was a different world; money wasn't used like we think of using it. Mr. McKinney took half of the corn for grinding it into meal. They used the barter system. There was one store and it was more of a meeting place for everyone than a store. The store wasn't open for business on Sunday, but Sunday was the busiest day. The men and boys would go to the store to trade, and moonshine was in the back room. Money was never used, but something of value was traded. Then men would trade cows, horses, and ox. The boys would trade guns, knives, and watches. Every day was about the same for me, except Sunday. Dad was home on the weekend, so he would do some of my chores, so I'd go down to the store. This was all the excitement there in Basin, West Virginia.

Carie McKinney got to be my best friend, although he was old enough to be my grandfather. I did a lot of trading with Carie, mostly watches. I did remember Carie brought seven horses to trade one Sunday. I don't remember how it turned out. I traded a small wagon I'd bought a few years before for a shotgun. Some people will tell you a gun of this type didn't exist. I know it because I owned one. It was ten-gauge dual barrel 36" long and had hammers like an old flint lock gun. When I went on my first hunting trip, I took my old shotgun not far from our house. I saw a squirrel about two hundred or three hundred feet away. I shot it, as I lay on the ground. I looked at where I'd shot the squirrel and watched it fall to the ground. I went looking, and I heard the rattle of dry leaves below a tree. I pitched a rock down there, and the injured squirrel came around to my side of the tree, about thirty feet from me. I shot it again, and all that was left was the tail. I was proud to show mother my first kill. But I learned that wasn't the gun for me. I traded it for a .22 riffle.

We didn't have a radio, but the McKinneys up at the mill had one. They invited me up one night to listen to the prize fight with Joe Lewis and a fighter whose name I can't remember. I saw a clock on the mantel, and Mr. McKinney could see I liked it. He asked me if I wanted the clock and of course I said yes. He said I could have it for a sack of potatoes and a pair of old men's dress shoes. I got the sack of potatoes and Dad's dress shoes. Since Dad wasn't home much, he wouldn't miss them. Now the McKinneys lived up the creek, maybe a quarter mile. The mountains in that part wasn't where you could have a wagon. They used a sled pulled by a team of oxen. One named Bailey and the other Buck. When their son George Orlie Brown Jr. would start driving the oxen, I could hear him yelling "get up" at Bailey.

One early Sunday morning, I could hear George start the team with the whole family in the sled on their way to church. I had just traded for my .22 rifle, and I wanted to show how good I was with a shot. Dad was home and hadn't been awake for long when I shot Mr. McKinney's chicken because it was in our garden, as George Orlie Brown Jr. came down the path in front of our house. I took the chicken, threw it in the front of the oxen. Mr. McKinney started yelling at me, and Dad heard the yelling so he said to Mr. McKinney he would pay for the chicken. About that time, I looked down at Mr. McKinney's shoes. I never knew what else was said because I left the scene while Dad was right behind me with a switch.

Back to the entertainment at Basin. There was a hangout—a cave in the woods close by where the boys would hang out, play cards, and drink. One night while the moon was bright we heard the boys fighting. There was a small stream of water in front of our home and one of the boys had been hit in the head with a rock. He was bleeding and came to the water to wash it away. He dropped dead then. He was a relative of the one who hit him. As far as I know nothing was ever said about the death.

I don't remember many outsiders in Basin. I only saw one man whom I knew was not one of us, because he had a dress suit on. I had taken a sack of corn to the mill to grind some meal, and as I was coming home, I had some conversation with this man in the dress suit. He asked about George Orlie Brown Jr.'s education. He was about two or three years older than me, but he had finished the third grade. He asked Mrs. McKinney about why he hadn't gone to school lately. She said, "I don't right full know." George was born the same day Mr. McKinney killed the opossum in the stump in the front yard. They didn't know which year he was born.

These were good honest people, just different in some ways. They didn't have money and didn't need any. After a hard day's work in the summer time when the sun went down, the bugs would come out. We would go sit on the porch with a metal can with some kerosene in it, soak a rag in it, and it would burn for a while. Then it would make a lot of smoke driving the bugs and bees away.

This is the way you plan what you'll do the next day.

Clocks: The Beginning of My Mechanical Engineering Career

THIS CLOCK WAS what my dreams were built around. Our cellar under the house was one for storing food for the winter. The other side was dirt, which was where I'd play with that old clock. It had weights for power and I did everything you could think of with that clock.

My friend, Carie McKinney, saw my interest in timepieces. He gave me an old clock with a wind-up spring. I got to thinking of everything that needed power. For the gristmill, which is powered by water, Carrie needed to turn his lathe, and I'd turn his lathe with a foot treadle from an old Singer sewing machine. I'd clean his watches. Carie would take a watch apart, put all the parts on a string, and I'd dangle them up and down in a jar of cleaning fluid. This would take two or three minutes. Then I'd put the parts in a box of sawdust. The sawdust wasn't from a saw mill. It was used for years before electric power. I still use it sometimes. Carie took an interest in me and taught me about all the parts of a clock. I'm sure I helped Carie too. He had his watch bench at a window when he could get the best sunlight, because he didn't get enough light from a kerosene lamp to work on a watch. I'd go back home and play with my clocks, until it got so dark that I couldn't see. But I'd go to bed dreaming about what I'd like to do some day.

School was much different at the coal camp. In Bud, West Virginia, we didn't live in the coal camp, but we went to the same school, which by most standards was a good education. I think I was six or seven when I started to school at Bud, West Virginia. The school at Basin, West Virginia, wasn't like any other "normal" school. We didn't have electric power at Basin, West Virginia, but we did have electric power at the school. There was one small light in the center of the "one-room" classroom and an electric pump to get water from the well for drinking and the toilet. There were approximately eight to twelve students at the school, from the first to ninth grade. I had no interest in school, none. I think I learned more from the Sears catalog while setting in the outhouse than I did at school. I'd look at all the tools in the catalog and dream what I could do and things I could make.

When I wasn't dreaming about tools, I was dreaming about helping Carie. While at school, I seemed to be the only student whom the teacher could trust to watch our electric power system, which was called a Delco generating power plant. It was operated by kerosene oil. There were some gages that you had to monitor. This was my job while the other students had classes. I didn't have that all the time, but I was happy when I got it. I think I got it more than anyone else. There were some students in junior high and high school. I was in the ninth grade at a high school. It was either mud or snow that kept the bus from running. It was a small school bus. We called it tatter bug.

I completed my ninth grade at Herndon High School. With all my interest with Carie's watch shop, I still had all my chores at home to take care of. Get the wood in, milk the cow, feed the chickens, and get the eggs in. One job I had that makes me wonder about was our cow had a calf, and the calf had to get its milk before I had to milk. I had to take the calf away from its mother, and the bigger the calf got the more work there was to do. The mud around the cow was a mess. I wore the same clothes to school, and how dirty my shoes must have been! The only thing was, I guess, everyone else was just like me.

World War II Starts December 7, 1941: Pearl Harbor Is Bombed

THE ONE NIGHT I'll remember was I was able to stay awake until the Grand 'Ole Opera was over at 1:00 a.m. That was December 7, 1941, and now the United States was officially in World War II. I was thirteen years old. We got a radio, which used a car battery. We didn't have any way to charge it when the power was used up, but Dad had a pickup truck with the same type of battery. Dad would come home on the weekend, parking his truck on a hill. He would take the battery out of his truck, which was fully charged with power. He put the radio battery, which is out of power into the truck. We had a radio for a week; Dad would drift down the hill just so that he could start his truck. Everyone was happy for another week. I did like country music on the Grand Ole Opera. The opera was in the state of Tennessee, which meant it didn't go off until 1:00 a.m. I'd listen till I'd go to sleep, which was before 1:00 a.m. and the radio would stay on and run the battery down.

I thought I'm a man now; I could stay awake. Dad could see the war is not coming to West Virginia. I think Dad wanted us to move to civilization again. Dad had cut stone to build a house while he stayed at the mine when he worked. Dad built a stone wall, a big one for the owner of a lumber company in Mullens. I was old enough now to do a man's work so we moved to Stephenson, West Virginia. This was about 1943, and I was about fifteen years old. I was fourteen when we moved, and I turned fifteen on the July 9 that year.

Stephenson, West Virginia: 1943

Due to World War II, everything was rationed. Ration stamps were provided in a war ration book. One needed ration stamps to buy food, shoes, and gas.

447306   CW

WAR RATION BOOK No. 3

NOT VALID WITHOUT STAMP

During the war years, life was so much different in Basin, West Virginia. I don't remember anything rationed at Basin, West Virginia, but the rest of the country was under tight rationing restrictions. Dad needed ration stamps for gas, but we didn't know about that. Now that we are starting to build, there was so much to do besides building a house. Our home will be about fifty feet from the main high way, Rt. 16, so we can't let our cow run like we did at Basin, West Virginia, and we had to build a pen for the cow and a place for chickens and pigs. Dad always made a living, and we never went hungry. We had our own milk, eggs, and pork. In fact, Dad always planted a large field of sweet potatoes, which I loved for breakfast with a half-pound of butter.

School was out and Dad was ready to build our home. I don't remember much about the framework, but I sure do remember the stonework. I guess it must have been about school time when Dad started the stonework. I mixed the mortar for every stone in the house and carried every stone to Dad to place in the wall. It seemed we were just getting started when it was time to go to school. I had to take some tests, and the school said I'd have to start in the ninth grade again. It didn't make any difference with me. I wasn't going to study anyway. Dad had told me many times "education isn't for us; you only need to work hard and be honest." Dad had one thing he always said to me—you're a dumb stupid idiot and will never amount to anything.

I don't remember ever doing one minute of homework for school. I was told by my Dad that it wasn't important. When I wasn't doing good in class, I was told I could go to a trade school for half a day, so I liked that, mostly because half of the time was on a bus going to Pineville High for trade school.

Life at home wasn't the average home life. In fact, while I'm writing about my history, I remember many details about my life, but I don't remember anything about my sister, or my brother, Garman, who was about four years younger than I was. The only thing I remember about my brother, David, was I had him on a bicycle and he got his foot caught in the wheel and cut his foot. The house was finished. It was never a home, just a shelter and a place to eat.

Living in Stephenson was a different world than at Basin. I had to walk one mile to catch the school bus, and walked seven miles to Mullens to school. Every day after I got home, I had to help Dad build our house. Dad said education is for another class of people, so not having to study was all right with me.

At the age of fourteen, I was trying to learn what the rest of the world is about, and I knew I had a lot to learn.

Life at Stephenson was much different than Basin. In fact, I believe life at Stephenson was different than any other coal camp. There was a group of boys who didn't like me because I wasn't one of the coal camp kids. Every time that first year I had to go to the company store for something, the boys would want to fight. They stole my cap, they hit my dog, and I had a hard time staying out of a fight. I couldn't win anyway. I had started to school, and since the boys who belonged to the gangs didn't go to school, I felt safe. I found the people at Mullens so much different from the coal camp. This caused some problems with the teachers. The kids from the coal camp said the teachers at Mullens treated them differently. The kids who came in from all the other coal camps felt the teachers thought more of the city kids than the Mullens kids.

P. Allan Hill, sixteen years old (on left).

"You Owe Your Soul to the Coal Company Store"

⌘

WHEN WE NEEDED something from the Stephenson Coal Company Store, I'd have to walk. All we ever bought from the store was flour, sugar, and kerosene lamp oil. This trip to the store was something new. It seemed no one had any cash, but "coal company scrip." Scrip was a type of company currency. This way you can't leave your job, if you owe the coal company money.

The method in which scrip worked was when you buy something at the coal company store, you go to the window at the office with your scrip card and ask for the scrip you want. The payroll clerk at the coal company office looks at your work record and the work planned at the mine and decides how much scrip he can give you. If you asked for ten dollars in scrip, he would record ten dollars on your scrip card and then give you ten dollars in scrip in the form of a coin from Buckeye Coal and Cook Coal Company. You can spend that scrip at the company store. You can't get more scrip than the hours you have on your scrip card.

Dad wouldn't let us get scrip. We paid cash and things at the company store was higher than that at town. The company store would take cash, but they wanted you to get scrip. I don't remember us ever having a scrip card. Dad did not want to be in debt to the coal company and he tried to use all cash he could. We did our food shopping at Kroger's, which was a great big store. It was big to me. Kroger's used cash, and I don't think many of the miners at Stephenson had cash. They used scrip from the coal mines.

Life as a Fifteen-Year-Old

—————— ✂ ——————

I GOT THROUGH the school year at Mullens High. I was sent to a "trade school" half a day, which I loved. School is out and I wanted a motorcycle. Motorcycles cost a lot of money for some reason. I've always found a way to make money and lose it too. Now, due to the war, food was rationed and a friend was raising rabbits and selling them to the Piggly Wiggly store at Mullens. He sold me a pair of rabbits and I got started. At one time, I think I had five hundred rabbits. I was making money, not a lot, but I was only fifteen years old.

Now that school is out and the house is finished, I got a job cutting timber. A timber is a part of wood that is used to hold the rock in the coal mine from falling. Each mine has a different seam height, so the mines ordered the length they needed. So, we were cutting timber 38" long. These were days before the chainsaw, and we used a two-man cross-cut saw. If you didn't have a good partner, the job could work you harder. My pay was one dollar per day. I worked thirty days without any pay. Dad didn't think that was right so he went to Rhodell to see Mr. McKinney. He was from the McKinney family from Basin. Mr. McKinney said he couldn't pay me because the coal companies hadn't paid him, and the excuse was that he would pay me soon as he gets paid. Dad saw thirty chickens in his chicken lot, so Dad said, "I'll take the chickens." That was one big mistake that Dad made. His chickens had some sort of a sickness. Our chickens got sick and we lost most of them. My rabbits got sick and I lost most of them. Since I was selling them for food, I lost my business.

I'd wanted a motorcycle and I found one I could afford. It was a 1928 Harley Davidson for fifty dollars. The bike was at a coal camp called Tipple, West Virginia. I don't think the town is there now. It was close to Saulsville, West Virginia. Just the other side of Mabin, West Virginia. A friend and I went to pick it up. I think I was about fifteen then. I had fifty dollars from my rabbit business. I got on the bike and rode to the top of the hill to Saulsville when it stopped. My friend and I pushed the bike to the top of the hill. We thought when I started down the other side, it would start, but no luck. I left the bike there. My friend had a pickup to go back and take it to the motorcycle shop in Preston, West Virginia. I got to know the Harley Davidson shop in Williams, West Virginia, in the years to come. Anyway, the motorcycle could not be repaired, so another loss. Maybe I had learned from Dad.

I didn't like to lose.

I had been telling Dad how bad I wanted a motorcycle. One morning just before the school was out for summer time, Dad asked, "How bad do you want that bike?" I told Dad, "I want it bad."

I have always been driven to achieve a goal.

Now my life with Dad was somewhat different than in the years before. Dad would take another job after work hours. He needed my help and he wouldn't take a job unless I could be his helper, at full pay even when I was only fifteen. But Dad was always in demand, and I had to be a part of his project with full pay. So, I had a few dollars, but this bike this time wasn't cheap.

I'm now fifteen and school was out. I would be sixteen in July. You didn't need a driver's license for a motorcycle yet. For this bike, I had to perform some hard work for Dad. The church at Stephenson in Devil's Fork had to be rebuilt and raised up and I had to dig out the basement. My job was to get railroad ties enough to crib up the church, and in my spare time, I can help Dad with the basement. I can't recall exactly, but the bike cost $400 as I could remember, but that can't be true because the bike would cost like $50,000 now. So anyway, whatever it was, there was a check on the breakfast table next morning. The first thing I did was go to Beckley and buy my motorcycle.

The railroad had just replaced ties and left the old ties along the creek. In this area, there was a river. We lived one mile east of Devil's Fork along the river. The sun didn't shine where we lived, but only for three or four hours a day, because there was a steep mountain. A railroad track was cut out of the side of the mountain. So you have a mountain on the west side, a railroad at the bottom, a river, and our home along the river. So you can see why the sun didn't shine at our house as there was a steep mountain on the south of the highway Rt. 16. My job was to get these railroad ties, over a hundred to crib up the church. I'd pull a tie down the hill from the track and put it in the water. I'd get three or four ties. I tied a rope around them and as they are tied end to end, I'd pull them down to the church. Each day I found that the length I had to pull them was increasing. The water was around twelve to eighteen feet deep, so I'd pull them down the river to where I'd carry them over to the church. Everything was OK until I had to carry a wet tie up a small hill and across the road to the church. The weight of a wet railroad was around 250–300 pounds. After eight hours working at this job, I didn't ride the bike all summer.

When Dad said work was finished for the day and I had some time off, I went home and I'd throw my lunch box over on the ground and lay down beside it for a while!

Maybe some people would say Dad mistreated me, but I only thought of it as a job I asked for. Now at the time I write this, I am eighty-eight years old, and I really believe my health is great at this age because of that job. One thing I know Dad would never ask anyone to do something he wouldn't do. I'm not the only person to say Dad was a superman.

I heard the miners say Dad had a block of steel weighing nine hundred pounds sitting up on a set of horses. Dad would lie down and lift the nine hundred pounds up a few inches off the horses. Dad expected me to try to do anything he would do. The house we built as soon as we moved to Stephenson had a windowsill in a window at the top of the house. Dad put the stone windowsill on his shoulder, went up a wooden ladder carrying the stone, and put in place where it belonged. I guess that stone weighed over four hundred pounds. What worried me was what if that ladder would break.

When school started, I got a job at Kroger's store, doing whatever someone thought they needed. I remember one Saturday when I came in and then was some sort of a problem. I was told to keep out of trouble. The employees wanted to strike for the union. They wanted a wage increase. You wouldn't believe what they asked for. It was a one cent increase. They were making thirty cents per hour and wanted thirty-one cents. That afternoon, we went to work, and I got the thirty-one cents per hour too.

My job later was in the feed department to load large sacks that weighted one hundred pounds. The feed department was run by a friend, Mason Wood. Mason was about four years older than me. He was discharged from the navy because of injuries in the war. So, it's my job to do the work. I liked Mason. One Saturday Mason got a jar of "Red Top Malt" and made something to drink, often heating it up. I realized the first drink I took was something like whiskey, and if Dad smelled that on my breath, he'd kill me. This was an accident, and I had nothing more to do with it. I got off work at 10:00 p.m., and I walked home seven miles so that Dad wouldn't see me.

Mother liked my job at Kroger's feed department. I'd save people a special sack of feed if they would save me the sack so that mother could make our clothes. The feed company had beautiful designs in their material. A box of washing powder might have a set of knives and forks, and the customer needed two or three more boxes to complete. Dishes and other items were available; of course, that was the way it was during the war.

Many items were rationed, like lard, butter, coffee, and many other things, and of course gas. Farmers got extra gas stamps because of use of gas for equipment on the farm. I had farmers who wanted me to save them a special sack of feed and they would give me a five-gallon gas stamp. This is for something I'd have gone to jail had the law found out.

Our home was not in the coal camp. We lived one mile from the camp. No one else lived between our home and the coal camp.

I'd never seen a loaf of bread sold in a store until I worked at Kroger's.

Now that I'm working at Kroger's, I'm seeing things that I didn't know existed.

When I did go to the company store for something, there was a group of boys who wanted to fight. They took my bicycle, I hid it, and they took my cap and threw it in the river. I tried not to let them think it bothered me that much. While working at Kroger's, I'd go get lunch at the only restaurant in town. So, I got to know people there.

One night about eight of the boys from Stephenson, the ones who had been making trouble when I went to the company store and Stephenson, saw me just as I got off work and asked me if I wanted to go eat with them. I thought maybe I can make friends with them after all. I didn't like these boys, but what will it hurt to go eat with them. I didn't know about these boys. They only worked as a gang. We went into the restaurant, and I ordered a sandwich. They got a bill, finished eating, and just got up and walked out, leaving me sitting there. To this day, I don't know why I did what I did. It was not the way Dad taught me to be. But I did get up and ran out the door with them. I knew the area around Kroger's so I ducked under a pair of steps while the restaurant manager ran over top of me and never saw me. A few minutes later, while thinking about what I'd done, I went back and paid the bill for all the boys.

With the money from Kroger's work, I could buy a good opossum dog. I was proud of my hound dog and was anxious to go hunting with my opossum dog. I'd talked to one boy in Stephenson who said he'd like to go with me some night. I went to his home to ask him, and his mother said he was down at the church. Now at this church, as with many other small churches in the South, the boys would congregate just outside the church to see the cute girls as they came out. Well, I went down to the church looking for my hunting friend. Now I've only been back in civilization for a couple of years. But it didn't seem right to me that these boys should hang out near a church lot. I walked over to ask him if he would go hunting with me. But before I talked to him, one of the twins who were named Richard and Robert McKinney (they looked so much alike that it was said their Dad couldn't tell them apart) took his cigarette lighter and started burning my dog's tail. I asked him to stop, and he did it again. I called him a bad name, and he hit me and knocked me in a ditch beside the road and stabbed me just over the eye. I lay there bleeding. The boy whom I'd come to see went into the church to get Dad. I didn't know Dad was in there, so he came out and took me to Beckley to the hospital to get stitches. I was lucky it didn't bother my eyesight. I can see what a bunch of bad boys can do. They just look to see what bad they can do. The boy whom I'd wanted to go hunting with had gone to Virginia to work in the shipyard that week and it was his first day home. I overheard one of the group of boys say this boy was trying to make out with a girl who belonged to him. A twin said as soon as the boy

39

comes out of the school, we'll jump on him. I went around back of the school and looked up this boy. They were going to jump when he came out of the door of the school. He said, "I'll take care of them. You just watch." So that's what I did. I ran back around to see the action when he came out of the door. I didn't expect to see what I saw. The boy came out the door, and a twin went toward him, but he had a knife. This boy stabbed the twin three times in the head and cut his neck ear to ear. He had a light sweater on, and it was cut all the way around the twin's stomach. I helped carry the twin to where he could lie down. Would you believe the knife was so dull that there wasn't a lot of damage done? There were forever scars so the twins were never identical. The twins' family wanted the boy who cut the twin to go to jail. Dad had something to do with going to court for the boy, and the McKinneys didn't like Dad.

Anyway, it was almost bedtime and Dad started to whip me and I started to run. Dad threw a stick of firewood at me and hit my left elbow and broke it. He had to take me to the hospital to get it set and have a cast applied. He made sure asking me not to tell anyone how it happened. The odd thing that happened about that was when it was time to remove the cast, I felt the arm was as strong as new. I went to Dr. Steel at Mullens and he said, "You go home and cut the cast away. Then you get a sling for your arm for one hour on and then one hour without the sling." I was on my motorcycle. I left the doctor's office feeling good, and everything was OK. So, I got halfway home about half-a-mile and I thought I'd cut this thing off now. So, I did, and, boy, I was surprised when my arm dropped down without any strength at all. I got the motorcycle started, but I couldn't lift my hand up to change gears. I got the bike in the second gear and that was the gear it stayed through the rest of the way home. Dad and mother never knew I was the one who removed the cast. Now I can appreciate how weak a limb can be when not used for a while.

A Teenager in a Coal Mine

Dad was the boss of the mine car shop. He said he would give me a job after school where I could make more money than Kroger's. This was also close to home. Only job was whatever someone wanted me to do. I would sweep the shop after work. After work hours, I'd check the mine car wheels to see if they needed greasing. The one job I had to do was awful. It was drying sand. When the sand was dried, it was put in a container where the motor man would fill his boxes on the motor full of dry sand. The sand was used to put on the truck at the wheel to get friction.

There was a large pot belly stove with something like a large funnel around the stove. I'd have to fill the funnel with sand, and as it got dry, I'd shovel it into the container. The dust was so bad you couldn't breathe. No one thought of something like a mask. I hated that job. The manager of the mine was Dad's boss, Mr. Roy Blankenship. I first met him when I was about five years old. He was my Sunday school teacher at Bud, West Virginia. I always thought he liked me. One Sunday he put straw in the bed of his pickup truck and took the Sunday school boys down to a town in Virginia and bought us some ice cream. That was my first ice cream. That was a really great thing to be treated like that then. He has always been a superman in my book, although one time he wasn't proud of me. Back to the sand drying. I have some real strong feelings about that job. The mine is like a road, highway. It had steep hills and the motor car used the sand put under the motor wheels to give it friction. The part I got to be thinking about was the motor operation has the sand grounded into a silica, which went right back on the face of the operator. It was not healthy. Many motor operators ended up with black lung problems.

Back to the reason why Mr. Blankenship wasn't proud of me. We had a great motor man for a car in the mine and each motor man has a break man. The great motor man was a young man by the name of Mr. Hess. I'd watched him go to pick up a line of coal cars. He ran a big twenty-ton motor. I'd watch him go to pick up the cars, maybe one hundred ahead. He would go full speed with that twenty-ton motor, and when he got close to the cars, he would reverse the controls to make the motor go in the other direction. Just as the break-man dropped the pin connecting the motor to the cars, his motor was at this exact moment going with the group of mine cars. Hess was maybe in his thirties and didn't go to the service. His service at the mine kept him out of the military. My part-time job after school was to grease the car wheels. I had maybe twenty cars to grease, and now I must put them on the side track so they would be ready to use. I had a small motor, at one time. It was a battery-operated motor, but it had been changed to an electric motor. It was only to be used what I was using it for. It had a sprocket chain from the electric motor to one set of motor wheels. I had just completed my grease job. I had all these mine cars pushed into the side track. Well, not realizing I got all these cars pulling me down this track, I thought I'd stop my motor by reversing the controls. The sprocket chain broke and these cars were now pulling the motor, while I was trying to set the breaks. By this time ten mine cars had gone over the stop at the end of the side track. They ended up in the river. I was given orders from Mr. Blankenship to keep off the motor. I had some experience at going inside the mine. I had to go inside a few times with welders and faced different problems.

I skipped school a few times when they had a special job. The war effort was more important than school; half of my day was at the trade school. The jobs I had were something like standing by with a fire extinguisher, just in case it was needed. Working in the mine was like play to me. Sometimes I'd get a scooter to ride. The mine was so low that you couldn't stand up, so there was a special scooter you would put your knee in a pad, take hold of a handle in front, put it on the track, and away you go. On one trip I was going fast and ahead was a curtain, a material seal to make the air in the mine go the way they want it to go. I couldn't stop so I went right through the material. Of course, it had to be replaced right away. Those scooters weren't made for a sixteen-year-old kid. They weren't made for play.

While I was working at the mine, half the time there was one man in the office. His job was called dispatcher. Maybe there were eight or ten motors in the mine at the same time. The dispatcher talked all the time on the phone to each of the motor operators. He knew where each one was and how long they will have to stay there until another motor passes by.

This was a sad part of my coal mine experience. That day was the last day before the miners' vacation. The dispatcher told Mr. Hess to wait where he was until the motor coming in goes past. Mr. Hess knew he must wait there at this hour every day and knew it took the motor fifteen minutes to pass. I've got all these coal miners wanting to get home so that they can get ready to go on vacation. Mr. Hess that evening had what you call the man-trip "transportation." Mr. Hess knew from previous experience that I can make it to the next stop in ten minutes, so I was going for it. Mr. Hess had his big twenty-ton motor pulling several mine cars with a lot of miners wanting to get out of the mine. This was approximately ten miles back in the mine "mountains." The coal seam in this mine was five-feet high. The steep track caused Mr. Hess's motor to reach a speed of around twenty-five or thirty miles per hour. Mr. Hess's motor hit the motor coming in "head on." There were seven miners including Mr. Hess who were killed. You can't imagine how that steel can bend on a big piece of equipment like two bull dozers hitting head on at over twenty miles per hour.

At the age of sixteen or seventeen, my temp job was to remove an old building, which was about one hundred years old and the coal dust was awful. That was on a hot day when for some reason, I began to think about my future. This isn't what I'm going to do the rest of my life. What can I do? I can't be a schoolteacher. I can't be a bookkeeper. These are respectable jobs that I want, but no way without an education. My mind turned to how happy I was while working with Carie McKinney on watches. Now that watch repairman at the watch shop in Mullens seemed to be a respectable job.

Someday maybe I'll be able to do that. I know I'm not dumb like Dad tells me. I just need a chance to do better and I'll never be satisfied with myself until someday I can try. It took that dirty, hot job to make me think about my future. School hadn't started yet. When Dad and I got into an argument about something, it was at a moment when I felt I couldn't live like this any longer. Dad always called me an idiot, and it hurts when you know you're not an idiot. I tried my best to do everything I did. I decided to leave home, because there wasn't any love there anyway.

I was only a slave to Dad when he needed something. One thing I can't understand about my leaving home. I didn't take my motorcycle. I started to walk. We lived at Stephenson, West Virginia, at the time. I don't have any idea how I got to the eastern bottom of Garwood Mountain. I just remember I was walking when I saw a coal train pull out from a mine. I jumped on a car, and it got going too fast for me to get off so I stayed on it till we got to Princeton, West Virginia, rail yards. I don't think anyone even saw me. The ride was approximately thirty miles. I spent two nights sleeping in a school bus, which was parked besides the road, but I can't remember when I went to the bathroom or what I ate. I guess I had some money, but I'd never seen a motel so I didn't even think about one. Now, I went past that area where an old bus was parked, and I wonder what I must have been thinking back then.

That was a low point in my life. There was no one you loved and no one who loves you.

I can't say I had good thoughts about anyone in my life. Grandma Hill hadn't been close as do a lot of grandparents. Grandma Hill lived about two or three miles from where I was sleeping in a bus. I ended up there because it was close to where I ended up on the train ride. Some way I ended up at Grandma Hill's. Dad came to get me. I had no idea how Dad knew where I was. There wasn't a phone in your home back then. It's best to forget some things or in my case I don't remember.

This is something that happened on the same tram road where Buzz, Bill, and I took a sled ride down the slate dump. I'd just finished my part-time work at the mine. I think it was 1944. I got news about a friend at Bud, West Virginia, who got killed. We had been the best of friends. He could keep off the ground as he swung from tree branch to tree branch better than anyone of us boys. His name was Clinton Lambert. Clinton and some of his sixteen- and seventeen-year-old friends found something to play with on this old tram road.

There had been old coal mine cars left on the track. We boys got in and drifted down to the car, which was turned over at the end of the track. On the next ride, Clinton thought he would jump off before it hit the car. Clinton jumped, lost his footing, and fell across the track in front of the car he was riding. The mine car was approximately two to three inches high off the ground. The car stopped in the center of Clinton's chest, and his head was just about cut away. Every child around the miners had been told to keep away from the tram road. We were told to keep away from the slate dump as it was dangerous, but we didn't listen. I went to Clinton's funeral at Bud, West Virginia, and Mrs. Lambert asked me to be a pallbearer. I said I can't because of my clothes. I'd never had a pair of trousers. I had a pair of overalls and a pair of "brogues" for shoes. At the age of seventeen, I was ashamed of my clothes, but after I said I couldn't, I wish I could have helped Mrs. Lambert. It was a short time after that the school started and mother gave me some money and told me to buy some clothes.

School started at Mullens High. It was September 1945. I found myself back in the ninth grade. I didn't think much about it; I couldn't complain because I had never turned a homework paper in. I hadn't ever turned in a book report while at school and I could see students who acted as if they had known everything. How my life would be if I could think that way.

There was one girl who tried to help me in a class, and I thought how wonderful life would be if I could feel as free as that girl. Why would she want to help me? She didn't have much success, because the school asked me to go to trade school half a day and the little girl didn't have classes with me anymore. When the school year was about halfway over, I got a call from the principal's office. He said I haven't made a passing grade since I was there. Only once in Health I made a "C." He asked me, "What do you want to do with your life?" I had the motorcycle and found a book about motorcycle riding. The book belonged to my motorcycle riding friend, Keith Roop. Someone planned a trip to South America.

The principal called me in to discuss my grades and asked me what was my ambition in life. I said I wanted to ride a motorcycle to South America. He said, "I think you should start now."

All I could think was that I'd like to get as far away from home as I can get. This story about the trip to South America involved a man who had to go across some fields with water. He made a raft from logs and got a water buffalo to pull the raft with the motorcycle to the other side of the lake. Maybe this isn't what a normal person would think of, but I found it would be exciting for me. No one would be telling me what to do. I was thinking I wanted to be independent.

Someday I want to be my own boss. I wasn't sure; I just wanted to be away from home. I felt free when I was riding my motorcycle. At seventeen and a half, life can be complicated when your life at home isn't good, and life at school isn't any better.

US Navy

I HAD ALWAYS dreamed of a life like some other people I'd seen—nice car, big home, and happy people. This wasn't my life, but all I could do was dream. In my mind, I really thought all this could be mine. Someday, maybe I was dreaming, but I thought if you work at the right things hard enough, life will be better someday.

I left school and in a few weeks, I rode my motorcycle to Bluefield, West Virginia, to join the navy. The weather was so cold when I stopped to get gas. It took me a long time to get my frozen fingers out of my glove. When I got to the recruiting office, I was told I'd have to have my Dad sign for me. So, I went back a few days later and joined the navy for two years.

I'm not sure how and what other people think, but I felt this was just what I needed. I loved boot camp. While others didn't want to take orders, I could see the harder I tried, the better I'd get along.

I can still remember the feeling I got at boot camp! When I picked up my clothes and supplies, I joined the navy in the first week in January 1946. The war had been over four months before. Many times I've thought, How could I get into the service with no education at all? Maybe because the war was over, many men would be coming home, and the navy would take anyone just to replace the ones coming home. My enlistment was for two years.

When I left home, my life turned completely around. Before, nothing ever happened good except getting a motorcycle. After I left home, everything was one hundred times better for me than anyone else. Maybe it was because I appreciated it so much more.

I thought boot camp in the navy was fun. Some of the boys from New York couldn't carry the field backpack on some of the hikes and I'd take theirs and carry mine as well just to show off. I didn't get tired at all. I don't remember writing home while in boot camp, or much while in the navy. I remember how proud I was because our boot camp unit got three extra days leave because we were number 1 out of approximately twenty units. I don't remember what I did while home on a ten-day leave other than ride my motorcycle.

My last day home on leave I rode my motorcycle to Rhodell, West Virginia, and parked it as I was talking to some friends. A man walked up and was talking about how good he could still ride after losing a leg in an accident. Without asking me, he jumped on my bike and took off down the road. A few minutes later, someone drove up and asked if that was my motorcycle that was wrecked down the road. The man on my motorcycle started to turn around and he killed the engine and was trying to start it. Now the bike was just off the road but stopped. A pickup truck came along and ran into the back of the bike. The back wheel was under the seat. The man driving the truck was drunk, and he just happened to work for Dad. He asked me not to call the police and said he'll take care of it. I went back to camp the next day, but the motorcycle was taken to the motorcycle shop in Princeton, West Virginia, and repaired like new. I never saw the bike after that, but Dad sold it for more than I paid for it. I don't remember how I got back to Camp Perry in Williamsburg, Virginia.

I don't think I was at Camp Perry except for a few days and got orders to go to Shoemaker, California, somewhere near San Francisco. This is one of the things that happened in my life that I can't explain. While at Shoemaker waiting for more orders, I looked on a bulletin board and saw a name Ellis Riffe, from Crab Orchard, West Virginia. My family had moved to Crab Orchard while I was in boot camp. I didn't know anyone, but I would've liked to have known someone when I came back home. I found Ellis and we talked. He was coming home after the war and I was going overseas. Ellis said when I got home to look for him and he would show me around Crab Orchard, West Virginia.

I was at Shoemaker for less than a week and I was sent to Treasure Island waiting to be shipped overseas. While at Treasure Island I had a very interesting thing to happen. There was a prisoner who escaped from Alcatraz, which was only a stone's throw from Treasure Island. The navy gave us a .30-06 rifle and had us stand guard at the edge of the island in case the prisoner swam from the rock over to the island. No one ever saw anyone swimming.

After about thirty days, I was shipped out to Guam. After the ship was out to sea an hour or two, I got so seasick that I wanted to die. That sickness lasted two or three days, and believe it or not, I learned to love rough water. In fact, the rougher the water the better I liked the ship ride. I learned to like the ship rolling when the water got rough.

I loved the navy. My first duty went on one flight taking some oil barrels to the island not far away. I spent most of my time picking coconuts and whatever I was asked to do. I don't know if I could have stayed at Guam or not but, we didn't have enough water to drink when you wanted it. I was asked if I wanted duty on a ship just off the Guam Island where they have ice cream, you can take a bath every day, and it had all the water you wanted.

I think I was in Guam a month. While there I was told the navy didn't want me in the navy with a two-year contract. I'd have to now take a discharge or the navy would sign me up for four years for $500. I chose the discharge, but it wasn't available till I got back in the States to a discharge station, which took a while. I spent one year, ten months, and ten days of my two-year contract. I took my duty on the ship just off the Island of Guam. It was big, very big. It was the most important ship in that part of the world. It was the flagship of the fleet. We had an admiral and he had eight captains for his aides. I was assigned to the Navy Air force. We didn't have any of the duty the sailors had. We were called Air Dales.

We went up in the Sea of China on the USS *Boxer CV21* for our first tip. Then for July 4, we sailed to the Philippines to the capital city of Manila. I guess this was the most exciting time ever. The Philippines was gaining their independence on July 4, 1946. Because the USS *Boxer CV21* was the admiral's flagship of the fleet, all the important ceremonies took place aboard our ship. Our ship couldn't get into Manila because of the ship wrecks in the water just outside of Manila. As I looked from the ship toward Manila, I thought I saw many telephone poles stick up out of the water; however, they were the masts of the ships that had been sunk.

TOP: Our ship the USS *Boxer CV21* aircraft carrier was the pride of the US Navy.
This photo was taken in front of the Golden Gate Bridge. Maybe I was on-board?
BOTTOM: The July 4, 1946, ceremony onboard the USS *Boxer CV21* aircraft carrier.
The ceremony was attended by President Truman, General McArthur, Admiral Nimitz,
and Admiral Halsey. The ceremony celebrated the Philippines' newly gained
independence from Japan. I was there!

After a couple days getting ready for the big day, with the Philippines obtaining their independence, there certainly was a lot taking place on our ship. Very few people on earth will get to see the excitement that took place on our ship that weekend. There were so many important people on board our ship. Our ship was the host of this big event. We couldn't take pictures, but I can remember how exciting it was even if I didn't get to Manila.

My duty on the USS *Boxer CV21* aircraft carrier was as a plane spotter. As soon as a plane landed on the flight deck, it would taxi to the elevator and must be lowered down to the hanger deck. This was where the plane was stored and maintenance was performed. As a plane spotter, I had to make sure it was cleared of any obstacles and would not get damaged. This was my first duty in the navy. There were eight or ten of us pushing the plane to where it belonged. I loved what I was doing. We had a sailor who was a warrant officer in charge. He looked different than most sailors, and he was from New York City. After a few weeks, the warrant officer came to me and said, "Looks like you are the only man pushing sometimes." Well, this was what I had been taught to do, what I'm told to do, and do my best. He said, "I want you to go topside and see an officer." I don't remember his name, but I had two good points: one, I did what I was told to do and did it and two, I was a little stronger in build than most. This new duty was a promotion for me.

P. Allan Hill (left) as a pilot rescue specialist and firefighter dressed
in his asbestos suit, onboard the USS *Boxer CV21* aircraft carrier (1946).

My new job on the USS *Boxer CV21* aircraft carrier was to be a firefighter and attend school at every port and learn about all new materials to fight with. I had to be strong because I had to wear an asbestos suit, which weighed approximately 80 lbs. while the planes were taking off or landing. I loved the excitement and saw lots of action.

Operations in 1946 onboard the USS *Boxer CV21* aircraft carrier.

Our ship was the US Navy's largest aircraft carrier. We got all the new navy pilots who were in training. This was sometimes the first time a pilot was going to land on an aircraft carrier. It was different than the practice they had to do on the ground. There were many who, when they saw that little boat down there, thought, "I can't land on that," and they couldn't pass as a navy pilot. Some who did come in had a little trouble, but they learned. My duty was most interesting and exciting. The back half of the deck was where the planes landed. There was a pilot at the end of the ship called the LSO, who used flags in his hands to wave the pilot onto the ship, on what direction to go to make a good landing. The LSO would wave them off many times and have the pilots try to land again. When the plane came in before the plane wheels hit the deck, the plane's tail hook would catch a cable, which was stretched across the deck and stop the plane. There were several cables, so if you didn't catch the first, the pilot would catch the four others. There were two men to disconnect the tail hook from the cable, a man on each side of the ship. I was there with these men at the aft part of the ship where all the excitement took place, and not every plane made a perfect landing.

After an aircraft crash *USS Boxer CV21* aircraft carrier (1946) (Photo: P. Allan Hill).

My job was being in the landing area in case I'd have to go in and get a pilot out of a burning plane. There were only four men at the aft end of the ship where all the excitement took place. I was like watching an auto race, and when there was a plane wreck, I was there up- close to see it. And, I did see many. One that did excite me was when an F-4/U fighter plane came in. The LSO gave the plane the landing OK but when the plane came in the ship, a large wave lifted the aft end of the ship up and the plane crashed and it's wing broke off because it landed so hard. (See the photo above.) The plane's tail hook didn't hook the cables so the plane turned upside down with one wing broken off and the plane slid up the deck toward me. I jumped over the side of the ship away from the plane. There was a cat walk for one to jump into, but there was a cook who wasn't supposed to be there and I jumped on top of him with my heavy suit. Anyway, I don't know if I hurt him or not, but one thing for sure there wasn't anyone in my way after that. I had to cut the pilot out of his safety belt and pull the pilot out first just in case the plane would catch on fire.

Every seaman wanted my job and to be an Air Dale, like me. All I had to do was stand there and watch all the fun. The ship's crew didn't like us because we had a better life than they did. The Air Dales had our own chow hall, and many things the sailors didn't have. The Air Dales didn't have ship duties.

Air Dales, like the rest of the ship's sailors, when off duty, sure did like to get drunk. They got drunk every night when they had the liberty. It's expensive to have fun. The boys never had money when they needed it, so I thought I'd help them. Believe it or not, I was the moneyman of that flight group. I would loan a man ten dollars for twenty dollars. In fact, I would take them to get drunk and charge them for bringing them back for duty the next day. I got to the point and figured a way to take two dollars every payday, which was every two weeks. The two dollars will buy your soap, toothpaste, and whatever you needed. I'd get my two dollars and wait for the boys to come by and pay me. If I didn't get my money on payday, it was hard to get later.

I was sending my pay each day to the bank back home. You wouldn't believe how many ways there was to make money in the service. I pressed their uniforms for money, and I polished their shoes, but the most I made was from the army. There were three thousand soldiers who had been discharged in the Honolulu, Hawaii, area, and they got their mustering-out pay there and our ship was their transportation home. Now they had cash and started playing cards. I saw so much money in one pot. I don't think a bushel basket would have held all that money. I was making money getting them food and drinks. I felt sorry for some, as they would go home broke.

I never took a drink, not even a beer while in the navy.

The USS *Boxer CV21* had liberty divided into two different groups: the port side group and the starboard side group. Starboard side got liberty first. I was on the portside and would get liberty tomorrow. There was so much excitement. Every sailor got drunk and caused a lot of trouble so there wouldn't be any liberty for the port side. So, all I could do was look. The ship was anchored about one mile away from Manila. The weather got rough that afternoon and the boat got waves of water into it. The sailors had to dress in their best uniforms for this. Now with the rough water, and a boat load of drunk sailors, it was a mess. The drunk sailors couldn't come aboard, so a cargo net was lowered down to the boat, and the sailors were loaded into the net like cargo material. They were brought up to the hanger deck and dumped out of the net like cargo. If you didn't have a friend to come and get you, you stayed there until you could get up. I'll never forget one person I saw in the group was the Catholic chaplain dumped out of the net like cargo.

There were a lot of exciting things that happened just because our ship was a big aircraft carrier. While in Honolulu we had to pick up some old planes and bring them to the United States. We had over two hundred planes aboard our ship. We picked up and had to secure them down, and what a job. You got a big PBY seaplane and under its wings you put a small fighting plane. One of the times I sure thanked the Lord for saving me. I was out on the end of the PBY plane wing, securing a line to the end of the wing. The PBY being a seaplane too, it had a pontoon at the end of the wing. I was out at the end of the wing lying on the pontoon securing the line when just as I finished and moved back on the wing when someone in the cockpit did something that made the pontoon to lower down. If that had happened while I was out there, I would have fallen to the concrete deck about thirty feet below. Anyway, sometimes you get nervous just thinking about it.

Our ship was docked, and the air force field was across the road from our ship. So, to get to the post exchange to get some goodies, we would catch a bus at our ship and ride all the way around the air field to the post exchange. Well, a couple of my friends said we just missed our bus and would have to wait a half hour for another. We could see our ship just across the field, so why wait? We started walking across the field and here come cops with red lights and they took us to jail. We had an executive officer to come and get us out of jail. Nothing more was ever said about it. In fact, it was about time I had been studying to get my GED. I got it after taking a test and then applied for my high-school diploma. So, now I could say I'd finished high school.

The navy life was very exciting for a young boy, and I enjoyed every minute of it. One exciting thing I remember was on Navy Day. We were in the bay in California where this big plywood airplane, Howard Hughes' "Spruce Goose" flew a few feet. It was the first and only flight that plane ever made. This was real history at that time.

I was an eye witness on November 2, 1947, when Howard Hughes' "Spruce Goose"
flew a few feet in Long Beach, California.

I got to go home on leave on three occasions. I took public transportation on one trip home and traveled back by train. Other than that, I thumbed or hitchhiked a ride. I loved that, and almost every time I made better time than on the train or bus. At the end of my enlistment in the US Navy, I bought a bus ticket because I had all my navy gear, and this was too much to hitchhike with. While getting ready to leave, someone broke into my locker the next morning and stole all my things. All I owned was gone, except the clothes on me.

I finally got home on December 17, 1947.

Home from the Navy: August 1947 to June 1950

———— ⌘ ————

WHEN I GOT home from the navy, it was a few days before Christmas. The first thing I had to do was buy some clothes. I had lost all my navy gear when someone stole everything I had, except what I had on my back.

I also had to buy presents for everyone for Christmas, so I was busy for a few days. My first thing was go see Dad at his work showing him my discharge. He said, "Mr. Blankenship wants to see you." He was Dad's boss. He was also my Sunday school teacher when I was about five years old. Mr. Blankenship said, "Now you have the GI Bill and you have to use it and go to school." My answer was, "I don't have a good education, so I can't get into school." He said, "You can go to a trade school and be an electrician or a plumber, and lots of trades that don't require a great education." At that point, I was not sure about school, or what I was going to do. Mr. Blankenship said, "If you will sign up for a school, I'll give you a job until your school starts." This was a turning point for my life.

I didn't know a lot about watches, but I'd learned enough from Carie McKinney to be interested, so I went to Mullen's Jewelry store to ask questions. I was told there were two places where you can learn to work on watches. Hamilton Watch Company in Lancaster, Pennsylvania. I went to check it out and found it's a small school, with only ten students and to get into the school, you had to be recommended by a jewelry store. The other was a school set up for GI students, which is where I checked in to. It was January 1, and the next class didn't start till August 1. I've got six months to work, getting ready for school. This job was as Dad's helper in the blacksmith shops. Dad and I had not really gotten along well before I went to the navy. I don't know who changed the most, Dad or me. As I watched Dad work and see how he managed other things after work, I thought we are a lot alike. Dad could do things with a piece of steel you wouldn't believe is possible. Then after work he would take on another job.

Dad bought an army jeep and a small trailer when he built a blacksmith shop in the trailer. He would go around other mines, get their cutting drill bits for the miners, and sharpen them for their next day's work. He charged two cents for each bit. I learned it wasn't the money Dad wanted, but it was to show people what he could do. As I write this I'm not sure, but I'm a lot like him.

My life is so much different now than it was before going into the navy. I didn't know what I'd end up doing. But my future is looking bright. For the first time, I've got a good job, not part-time. I'm making $7.21 per day and for the first time I'm not working for Dad, I'm working with him.

The first thing I needed was a car and some clothes. I bought a car. You couldn't just go and buy a new car. You had to order one, so I did. I found out it took nine months to deliver one. I bought a 1940 Chevrolet two-door 'coup. The original cost was $740, and I paid $1,300 for it. It was like new. The car belonged to a doctor's wife and had been well maintained.

I lost all my navy clothes when I started home, so all I've got is on my back. I went to a store and went "hog wild" buying new clothes. I bought some real nice dress clothes, something not many eighteen-year-olds had. Nice clothes and a car. I'd had trouble in school and there was a cute girl, who was the smartest in the class, who had tried to help me in schoolwork, and we exchanged letters a few times while in the navy.

So, I've got my new clothes and car. I asked the cute girl for a date. To my surprise, she told me her father wouldn't let her date a coal miner's son.

Another reason for my writing about my life is because of the blessings I've had. The Lord has looked over me in so many ways I can't explain; there isn't any way to explain amazing things.

A few days after the girl turned me down, I found the love of my life, Lila Horton, and it's now been sixty-four years ago. Just after I bought the car, I looked up Ellis Riffe, whom I saw at Shoemaker, California, a year or two ago. He said when I got to Crab Orchard, look him up, and he'll show me around. We met at the Crab Orchard Baptist Church for a Baptist Youth Fellowship group meeting. While talking to Ellis, I saw a cute little girl named Lila riding her bicycle up the road and I asked who she was. He asked me if I wanted a date. I said yes! Ellis told me, "I'll get you a date but I'm going to marry her." He got me a date, but her mother said Ellis would have to get a date and go along. My life until now had many ups and downs.

Life before the navy was nothing good. Home life couldn't have been worse. I took that cute little girl home after our date. When I met her family, I was in a state of shock to see that the

Horton family seemed to enjoy life. I hadn't even seen anyone at home smile about anything. I've said at first, I fell in love with her family before I did with her. Lila was fifteen years old, and I was eighteen on our first date. We had many more after that. I believe our love affair has been the best and maybe the longest It's now been sixty-five years and I hope there is a lot yet to come.

I'm now working with Dad. I'm thinking about school, but I'm not sure what it will be like. I just know it's going to start in six months. My work with Dad isn't bad. Dad seems to do more things where he needs my help and keeps telling me how much he needs me. Sure, it is different than it used to be when all he ever called me was "You are a dumb idiot" and "You will never amount to anything." I'd heard that a thousand times, and all I could do was cry because I always did the best I could do.

When I got discharged, the US government gave me money, which was called "52-20," or twenty dollars a week for fifty-two weeks, and these payments were designed to help new GIs settle down until they could land a job. I got my first and only twenty dollars. I got a job right away. I saw my friend George three or four months later who had been discharged the same time I was. I ask George, "Have you got a job yet?" and he said, "Why, I'm getting twenty dollars a week, so why work?" I told Dad the next day. Dad put his hand on my shoulders and said, "Son, that's the difference between a Democrat and a Republican." That was the first time Dad ever called me son, but I got the message. I've been a Republican ever since. I didn't know the difference between either political party, but in my way of thinking, I was proud to work for the money I earned. I know there are people who need help, but there are too many like George.

As I worked with Dad, I learned a lot. When I had to heat a piece of metal, he would say, "It's not hot enough" or "It's too hot." I hit the steel too hard or not hard enough, but my working with Dad is so different now than it was five years ago. I was beginning to learn blacksmithing, and Dad must have been the best, because I heard all the good things people said about his work. It's getting about time for me to start to school, Dad said you can't leave; you can't make $7.21 per day working on watches. I had already traded my car for a motorcycle and I knew I couldn't afford a car at school, but I could use my motorcycle to come home on the weekends. This bike was top-of-the-line new 1947 model. Dad didn't think trading the car for the motorcycle was a good idea, but I was old enough to do for myself.

July rolled around. Mr. Blankenship asked, "Allan, are you ready to start school?" I said, "Dad said I can't make $7.21 per day working on watches. I'm going to have to stay here and help him." Mr. Blankenship said, "Allan, you don't have a job here after July, and you're going to school." The school was Western PA Horological Institute and I had no idea what school would be like. I hadn't talked to anyone other than signing up six months ago. To start I found several students who didn't like school at first. We started with two pieces of wood ¼" × ¼" × 2" long. We had to take a file and cut designs into the wood, just like a picture. Now these kids who went there to learn to work on watches washed out and had to quit, and I always wondered what their family thought. At this point I'm there to do what I'm told to do, and somewhere, some time I'll learn to work on a watch. These families that sent their kids there to learn to work on a watch must have been disappointed. They should have stayed a little longer because the graduates got an old, big watch to take apart.

I had watched Carie McKinney work on a watch, so I had some idea. I learned how to repair a watch. As I moved into some advanced classes, I lost my interest in watches. I was amazed at the beautiful movements of a good watch. The mechanics of a movement meant more to me. I could see it keeps time, but how do you make those small parts. I finished watch repair class the first year. The second part was taking my class to become a master watch repairman. The teacher broke about every piece in the movement. I had to reproduce the broken parts. This required using tools, which I had to make. Our class name was called the "hairspring" class. At first I thought it was hard, but I learned the art and techniques to use the watchmaker's tools. It's odd the hairspring is almost like the wire strain gages that I wound for the rest of my career. I got into a class learning to make tools for making watch parts. It was an advanced class where you had to do more than make tools. I loved this so much I took six months more classes to learn more.

As soon as I learned to work, repair a watch, I found a way I could make some extra money. I got tools, a watch bench, and setup in my room where I could work on a watch. Some things in life are hard to understand. Back in 1929, there were very hard times. People then took all gold pieces to a "hock shop" (pawn shop). Many of these gold pieces were gold watches. The hock shop didn't want a watch, only the gold. They would remove the movement throw it into a basket as junk. I've gone to the hockshop to look at some movements. I've had as many watch movements as two hundred on a table for me to look at. I've bought as many as twenty or thirty at a time to take them home to clean them, buy a silver case for about two dollars or three dollars for the movement, bring them to Crab Orchard, and sell them for sometimes as much as twenty dollars or thirty dollars. I started this advanced class for making tools and it took much of my time, I had to stop working on watches. I found making things was more to my liking.

Maybe I took some of my interest in making things from Dad. After school, I set up a watch shop in the back of a store. I couldn't pay much for rent, so I got the space for 10 percent of my fee working on watches. The first thing we were taught in watch repair class was "Don't do any job you can't be proud of." Someone only wanted it to keep time in most of the watches I saw in Crab Orchard and didn't want me to change too much. I can't do that, and after one week the owner of the store said he needed my area, so I'd have to move. I wasn't disappointed. I was happy.

Things are not good in Crab Orchard at that time, so I got a great idea. I'd start a manufacturing unit to make grandfather clocks. I had some good ideas, which I thought might be better than most. I now needed to know woodworking to make the clock case. There was a class at the high school that taught cabinet carpentry.

US Air Force: 1950–1954

I DON'T REMEMBER if I was going to the school or coming back when a US Air Force recruiter stopped me and said the Korean War is starting and you will have to go. I was twenty-three years old. I told the recruiter I've already been in the service. He kept talking; he asked if I had been to school since the navy. I told him I'd been to a watchmaking school, and he got excited and told me what a good job he could get me in the US Air Force working on aircraft instrument. Now I'm excited this would be wonderful to add aircraft instruments to my resume.

So, without telling anyone I joined the US Air Force. The very next week I was in the US Air Force! I can't believe I did it, but my future at that time was bleak. Crab Orchard just wasn't the place for me to settle down. I had great plans for my future while in school. Crab Orchard wasn't the area where I could see my plans taking place. If I joined the US Air Force, I'll have time to think about my future, I'd learn about something, which might add to a better future for me. I can't explain why I signed up without telling the one I loved.

There are some things I can't explain. The next day was too late to change anything. Looking back maybe it was a crazy thing to sign up for the air force like I did. But the fact is, I can say now, it was one of the best things I've ever done.

My belief in life is if you make a mistake, you must live with it while working to correct the problem. The day after I signed up I was on my way to Texas, along with five hundred other service men who had reenlisted in the service. The first thing we learned was we are now in the new US Air Force. There isn't any longer an Army Air Force. We got our new uniform, a blue tie, blue belt, black shoes, and blue cap. There were five hundred of us waiting for orders. One boy went to Germany to work on cameras. I was sent to England to work on aircraft instruments. About a year later, the news was half of the 498 who went to Korea froze to death because they didn't have the clothes they needed for the cold weather.

I knew my sweetheart, Lila Horton (also known as Hutchie) and I belonged together. When I got my orders from the US Air Force and I got new uniforms, I also got a thirty-day vacation before going to England. Everyone wondered what service I was in; it wasn't a uniform anyone had seen before. What a wonderful thirty days! Hutchie still loved me, even after signing up without consulting anyone about going into the air force. I began to realize how much she meant to me, and how much we were in love. But I was in the US Air Force now and had to go to England. Who knew how long? Anyway, those thirty days made me realize I need that little sweet girl. We kept an honest love for each other by mail. I got to England by ship on August 1, 1950. I don't remember the type at all, but I do remember what the base looked like. It wasn't neat and clean like the navy.

While in England I worked on watches in a Quonset hut complete with a potbellied coal stove. Anyway, I got quickly adjusted to the air force life. There were two of us to work on watches. Nick S. from South Philadelphia. He couldn't work on watches so he was sent out around the base on a bicycle to wind clocks. There were approximately thirty time clocks to wind each day. These clocks were time clocks the English employees used when they came to work. I was an Airman Basic (one stripe) rank, lowest as you can get in terms of rank. In a few weeks of the war, some reserve units were called in to help. The watch shop got four new watch repair men. One was a bartender at home, another a farmer at home, and yet another a carpenter at home. The fourth was a fine watch repairman who had worked at Tiffany's in New York on only the best timepieces. They really knew nothing about a watch. When my commanding officer saw my background in watch school, he asked me if I could set up a class that would help the boys. I set up a class and had the boys servicing the watches. The commanding officer came in to see how things were going. He like my work and made me Airman of the Year on the base. I got three promotions (three stripes) out of that school. I was in good terms with my commanding officer and he said it hadn't been done on the base before, but he thought he could get the general to approve for Lila, my sweetheart, to come over and we could get married. It was a very happy day for sure!

P. Allan Hill and Lila Lee Horton are married August 1, 1951, in Warrington, Lances, England.

My lucky break came when a recruit joined our lab. By this time, I oversaw the lab. The lab had the four reserves. The recruit was a regular air force. The new regular air man became a very close friend. His name was Obe Thompson, a true Texan. Obe's background indicated that he was in his last semester at Oklahoma University in engineering. Oklahoma is a dry state, and Obe had some moonshine in his car when he had an accident. Oklahoma took it very seriously. Obe had in-laws in Texas with some pull. They got Obe off if he should join the US Air Force. He was sent to Burtonwood Air Force Base. He was assigned to work for me. He knew nothing about watches on the instruments. But he took care of me in everything that needed bookwork. I got the credit for many things he told me to do. Obe had a lot to do with me setting up the watch school. What a friend. I was promoted from private to four-stripe staff sergeant in thirteen months. I don't know anyone who made grade that fast. Obe helped me write the letters necessary to get my sweetheart to England, so we could get married. She arrived on August 1, 1951, and we got married that day, by the base Chaplin. That took a lot of paper work to get it done.

Hutchie enjoyed her plane ride from the States to England. We took our honeymoon trip to Germany. We flew out of Scotland. The weather was bad. I do mean bad. So bad a pilot next to us said, "I've been flying for years, and I've never seen anything this bad." We got to Frankfurt, Germany, and spent time bicycling. We bought a few things and then took a train through Belgium into the Netherlands. The train ride was not bad, but when we got to Amsterdam, Hutchie didn't enjoy the rest of the trip. When we got off the train, at approximately 11:00 p.m., the motel was a few blocks away, too far to walk and carry our luggage. The only money I had was traveler's checks, which I couldn't cash until the next day. I had two dollars in American money, which I was not permitted to have. Everyone wanted the American money, but it wasn't legal. Anyway, being desperate, I ask a cab driver if he would take me to the hotel for the two-dollar bill. He agreed and at the motel I told them I had travelers checks and could get the money for the motel at the bank next door. This was all right. What surprised me was about midnight, someone came to our room with some cash. It was the cab driver with some money. He said he didn't know how much the two dollars was worth and brought me back change. I bet Amsterdam isn't like that today.

The bad part of the trip for Hutchie was seasickness. As for me I enjoyed every minute out at sea. Her problem started as she got on the ship. This was a seven-hour trip across the North Sea of England. As the ship was tied to the dock, it was going up and down from the rough water. Hutchie got seasick before the ship moved out. This is hard to believe, but it was the roughest the North Sea had even been and the North Sea is known to be rough. In fact, an oil tanker broke in half that day. We had first class tickets so we had a nice area where we were. There were approximately fifty people in the first class. Everyone was sick except the bartender and me. People were sitting on chairs and couches and they broke away from the deck. Everyone was lying on the deck rolling as the ship would roll from side to side. I had to stay and watch Hutchie, but I wanted to go topside and feel the salt air. But no one was allowed topside because it was too dangerous. We did get home to Burtonwood, our air force base. Hutchie said, "I'm not going to fly in a plane again. I'm not going to be on another plane and ship. How am I going to get home?"

So many things in my life from this time only made me the happiest and most blessed person on earth. To start with, I found a nice home for us to live in. I was the first noncommissioned airman to get married to an American girl. There were a few officers who had their families with them, but I was first to marry an American. The airmen were marrying the English girls, some for different reasons other than love. Hutchie was nineteen and I was twenty-four years old. She had been to college a year while I was gone. My commanding officer asked Hutchie if she would like to have a job, watching children of the officers on the base. This was a government job and she had the status of an officer and I was her dependent. So, I could get anywhere the officers could go. I never took advantage of that, but my commanding officer asked Hutchie and me to go to Manchester University at night school and take some classes. We did, although I was never good at tests, and I was afraid I'd mess up. If you got married you got $5.75 more pay per day and could live off the base. Some found a girl who would go along with getting married just to get a free ticket to the States. When an airman married an English girl, they would move into the family home where the girl lived. They had to share the home, bath, and kitchen.

The English homes were small. Lila (Hutchie), the name by which all her friends know her, found a large home. So we had a nice bath and kitchen, along with bedrooms and a sitting room. The family who rented to us was like a mother and father to us. Mr. and Mrs. Wallington made

Mr. and Mrs. Wallington,
England, August 1951

wonderful friends. I felt sorry for them. They had a son approximately three or four years older than me and a daughter about my age. The son was in World War II in Germany and married a German girl. That wasn't good. The daughter married an American "yank." The English called us the "yanks." Their "yank" son-in-law went to the States saying he would take their daughter later. After a year, the daughter went to the States to find why he didn't send for her. She went to see an US Air Force lawyer to see what could be done. He solved the problem, he got them a divorce, and the daughter and the lawyer got married. Now both of their children had moved to the United States to live. So the Wallingtons took us in as their children. I've never been treated so well.

They loved Hutchie and me. After a few months, Hutchie, who did not like tea, asked Mrs. Wallington one morning, "Can you make me a cup of tea?" which surprised me because Hutchie didn't like tea. Mrs. Wallington slapped me and said, "What did you do that for?" As I was thinking, she said, "You got her pregnant" and I was surprised. Lila was pregnant with twins. Unfortunately, they both died soon after birth and sadly lived only three days. Mrs. Wallington was our only family at that time. We named the boys Dudley Allan Hill and Danny Calvin Hill. We didn't have a telephone and were only able to send a telegram home. We never called home the entire three and a half years I was there. The boys were buried in England at a US burial site.

Burying our twin boys, Dudley Allan Hill and Danny Calvin Hill, who died only three days after birth.

Mrs. Wallington was the only friend we had, and she was wonderful. We loved our life in England. We had a married life much better than the average airman. Mr. Wallington ran a large textile factory; they were not rich but much better off than the average English. Mr. Wallington had a Rolls-Royce limo to come and take him to work each day, and Mrs. Wallington needed to go shopping. They would come and get her. The only thing I can say is we were thankful for these good friends at that time in our life. The Wallingtons were the best and made us love England. We enjoyed several things because of the Wallingtons. One was when show people like Bob Hope would come to England to perform in cities like Liverpool or Manchester, Mr. Wallington would book the theater for his employees. Both Manchester and Liverpool were forty miles from Warrington, where we lived. One theater was forty miles east the other forty miles west. Anyway Mr. Wallington would rent five or six large tour busses for the employees to ride to the theater. Hutchie and I would get a seat with the Wallingtons up front in the bus. After the war most of all the English people were very poor. They would take a flask of tea and a sandwich on the bus and they were happy as anyone could be. From the way they sang and acted, you would think they were rich. We loved every minute except the loss of our two boys. We bought a MG TD series sports car. The dream of every young English boy, but he couldn't buy one. Every sport MG was sent to the United States for the American dollar. The car cost me $1,200. If it had been available to an English person, it would have cost him $2,800. You can see why not all English people liked the yank.

Polishing my new MG TD series sports car in England (1952).

We loved our MG sports car, and Lila Lee "Hutchie" and I visited some places in England and Scotland almost every weekend.

When it was time to go home, Hutchie said, "I am not going to fly in plane again" and "I'm not going to get on another ship." What were we to do? My orders instructed me to go home on a small, one-stacker the smallest transport ship, which was about the same size of a large tugboat. In the service, you follow orders. The airmen had different quarters from the women. Since I couldn't be with Hutchie, I worried about her getting seasick. But no worry. There wasn't a ripple on the water the whole trip. You could have taken a small rowboat all the way. But it was slow. The trip home from England to the States was nine days long.

In fact, on the trip home, we saw history. The SS *United States* was on its maiden voyage to and from England and was now on its way home to the United States and going in the same direction as we were. We saw the SS *United States*. This was now the biggest and best cruise ship afloat. We looked back and saw it going past us. It went by us like a speedboat. The SS *United States* made the trip in four days and it took our little ship nine days.

On the way home from England, We saw the SS *United States*.
The ship still holds the speed record for a transatlantic crossing by a passenger liner in three days and ten hours.

My orders were to go to El Paso, Texas Air Force base. While leaving New York, I had to pick up our car at the dock. It was my MG TD Series with about seven thousand miles all driven in England. We had a lot of baggage and the little sports car didn't have a lot of room. We put the top down so we could pack a little more luggage. The temperature was over 100 degrees Fahrenheit when we left New York at about 5:00 a.m. When we got to Lexington, Virginia, we had car problems, so a mechanic said he could take care of the car the next day. We got a motel for the night. This is a story hard to believe these days. The mechanic went to Virginia Polytechnic Institute, now known as Virginia Tech, just a few miles away. The mechanic was a teacher from Virginia Polytechnic Institute and made a new part and repaired the car, at no cost. That was the way the servicemen from Korean War were treated.

At about 12:00 p.m. we took off for home. Rain had been needed for a month and after we left Lexington, Virginia, approximately twenty miles, the rain came down. I could not get the convertible top to go up. I couldn't drive in the hard rain. Hutchie was worried about what her hair would look like when we got home. We got home and it was a great feeling to see family again. It was a short vacation for me because I had to go to El Paso, Texas, soon. The Studebaker car dealer saw my MG and wanted it. I didn't want to get rid of my little sports car, but Hutchie said it's not a family car. So I traded it for a four-door Land Cruiser Studebaker, which was a wonderful car. I kept it for eight years before trading it for another car.

When it got time for me to go to El Paso, Texas, I told Hutchie I'll go ahead and look for a place to live as we'll be there approximately seven or eight months till my Air Force time was up. I left the car with her, because I wouldn't need it on the base. This was my first problem with family. I had for years thumbed (hitchhiked) anywhere I wanted to go. So, I took my duffel bag up to the train station and sent it to El Paso. I planned to start the next day thumbing to Texas. Papaw Horton said, "No way is my son-in-law thumbing anywhere. It's too dangerous." So, he went up to the train station with me and picked up my bags and asked me to buy a bus ticket, which I did, but not because I wanted to.

I finally got to the El Paso, Texas, and got settled in, and I found a house. So now I've got to go back home to get Hutchie and the car. A friend said he can help me with a ride if I wanted him to. He said a friend of his is a big truck driver and if I wanted he would pick you up at the big truck station just outside the base, at 3:00 a.m. and he would take me to Texarkana, Texas, which was a 990-mile ride. So, I said yes. I got some early sleep before the trip. Before leaving on the trip, I called a cab for a mile ride with my luggage, and there were no cabs available because the weather was too bad. So, I took off walking. I had never been through a Texas sandstorm. It was so bad I had to walk backward with my coat over my head. I got to the truck stop, and the manager said there hasn't been a vehicle through here for hours. So, I waited a long time. After an entire day, a big car pulled in. The driver asked for a cardboard to put in the grill of his car. He got it and took off, got to the road backed up, and asked me, "Are you going East, soldier?" My first response was yes, but I asked him how far was he going. He said Raleigh, North Carolina. Boy, can you believe that? The reason for the question was while in the navy, thumbing through Texas I got to Sweetwater, Texas, and had to sleep under a picnic table. He was a navy officer going home in an emergency and had to get home soon and asked me to help drive because he had been on the road for a long time. He took me to the bus station at Raleigh, North Carolina so close to home. That was my last hitchhiking, if you could call that my last ride hitchhiking.

Now the trip in the new Studebaker was another story. It was Thanksgiving weekend 1953. On the Thanksgiving Day, the temperature was very warm and the next morning we had to pack and leave. I don't know what the temperature was, but there was twenty-seven inches of snow. A new car for me and I didn't know how it would handle the snow. The car didn't have snow tires. This was before interstate roads. I drove sideways, backward, and sometimes straight ahead. We got to Bluefield, West Virginia, and had to buy a set of chains to get up a hill. Believe it or not, on the other side of that hill, there wasn't any snow. It was good traveling all the way the El Paso, Texas. My duty at Burtonwood was the best anyone could have. Lackland Air Force Base was OK, but different in many ways. This was a Strategic Air Command Base, and everything was secret and you had to let the control room know where you could be reached every minute of the day or night.

Now at night sometimes I'd have to stay at the lab late. An officer learned I could do small parts work. A lieutenant colonel came to me with some drawings and asked if I could make him a model so he could use it to apply for a US patent. It took five hours, but I got it made for him. By the way that was the spring-loaded device that is used to clasp on any other thing to secure the object in place, such as the American flag on your lapel. This was the first time I had anything to do with an officer that high in rank. I liked him and he liked me, wishing me luck with my new life after the discharge.

My problem started at the base on my first payday. The noncommissioned officers club manager wanted me to pay dues each payday. My comment back to him was, "I don't drink, dance, and I don't want to join the club." He said, "You don't have a choice" and I told him, "I didn't think I should have to join the NCO Club." He wrote back and said I had no choice and owed dues for a few months by this time. Well, me being a person who didn't like someone telling me to do something which was to me completely out the line of being a good airman. I decided that I was going to join NCO Club.

Two days before my discharge, my commanding officer who was full bird colonel told me angrily that he was going to bust me down to Airman Basic and I wouldn't get money to send my wife and my household goods if I didn't join the club. He ordered me to pay all back dues to the NCO Club. The next day, the commanding officer Bird Colonel had to go home because of a death in the family. The officer I had been helping became the commanding officer in his place. So, the lieutenant colonel took his place while he was away and I called him to report my problem. I told him, "I can't afford that, but there must be some way I can get around this. Maybe you can help me? I know I'll have to pay if I can't get the NCO to sign me off. If you would please lay my papers aside until I can get NCO to sign off I'll sign up and pay my back dues, but I don't want to." He said OK, but before he can give me discharge, he asked me if all signatures are on the sign-off sheet. On discharge day I had a sheet with approximately sixty signatures to be affixed. I went everywhere and got all the signatures except the last one. I went to the NCO Club sometime after lunch, and there was a man at the desk who just filled in during lunchtime. He asked, "You don't belong to the NCO Club?" So I said here is the letter I sent to the general of the base, and it told all the reasons I didn't want to join. He signed the sheet. Of course, he didn't see the letter I got back from the general. Anyway, I walked over to the base officer to get my discharge and the first sergeant saw me walk out and he said, "I knew you couldn't get the discharge without joining the club and paying all back dues." I just laughed and walked to my car to go home. Good-bye air force.

Another thing I learned about how the Korean vets were treated was when I was stopped in Bluefield, West Virginia for speeding about 3:00 a.m. on the way home. The officer asked for my cards and to my surprise I had put them in a new pocket book I had bought in Juarez, Mexico, and it was in my luggage in the trunk. I'll have to get it out. He said, "You're now going home from your service in the Korean War. You be careful the rest of your way home." That was the end of my duty in the US Air Force.

General Electric Company: 1954–1961

NOW THAT I was out of the air force, I was not sure what my future would be, but one thing was sure—I'm not going to work on watches in West Virginia. With my schooling in horology, I thought I could get a job at the Gruen Watch Company in Cincinnati, Ohio, and went there to interview for a job. While sitting in the waiting room, an employee walked by and asked, "Are you looking for a job?" In my wildest dreams, I didn't think about a job at the General Electric Company (GE). Now this GE job wasn't just like job at GE. It was working on a team on a special project called Aircraft Nuclear Propulsion Department (ANPD). I wasn't told anything about the work I'd be doing at the time. I found I'd be investigated from head to toe. It was such a background check that I couldn't have qualified for the job if I'd had a parking ticket unpaid. The ANPD was conceived and started in 1950. The government wanted a jet plane, large-type plane that could stay in the air for days without landing.

P. Allan Hill working on a sophisticated instrument at General Electric.

The fuel system was a nuclear reaction, which would fuel the jet engine. The manager for the project was Dr. D. R. Shoults. Dr. Shoults was the engineer at the turbine department at GE in New York. The US government asked him to go to England and get all the technical details of England's jet engine. This was the beginning of the jet engine in the United States. In 1950, the US government asked Dr. Shoults to manage the ANPD, which started at Oak Ridge Nuclear Department before it headed to GE. As the plans grew, GE could see the work needed to be at the GE Jet Engine Department in Cincinnati, Ohio. The project was moved to Cincinnati in 1952. This was the most important government project in the world at that time.

GENERAL ELECTRIC
COMPANY

AIRCRAFT NUCLEAR PROPULSION DEPARTMENT

TELEPHONE VALLEY 7400 . . . . CINCINNATI 15, OHIO

October 18, 1954

Mr. P. Allen Hill
16 Hillsdale Avenue
Hartwell, Ohio

Dear Mr. Hill:

We sincerely welcome you to the Aircraft Nuclear Propulsion Department and are happy to have you as a member of the General Electric Family. I believe you will find that your choice of G. E. as an employer has been a wise one, and hope that your career with us will be very successful.

The field of nuclear propulsion of aircraft is, we feel, challenging and exciting, and the part which you play in helping reach the ultimate goal will be something in which you may take justifiable pride.

Your supervisor, Mr. Neuss, is the closest member of G. E. Management to you. He is very anxious to have you feel at ease in your new surroundings and to assist you in any problem you might have. As you become acquainted with your fellow workers, we think you will agree with us that General Electric is a good place to work.

Very truly yours,

D. R. Shoults, General Manager, ANP Department

DRS:bs

On August 5, 1954, GE sent me a letter informing me that my salary would be $74.15 per week. I'd have to pass a lot of tests before I could go to work. On October 18, 1954, I was told I had the job, but lots of information had to be studied before I could start to work in the Aircraft Nuclear Propulsion Department.

I was told I can start on the payroll now if I wished. It will take maybe three months to complete the security clearance before I could start to work in the lab. If I had something else I wanted to do until my clearance was obtained, I could do that or start on the payroll now. I had a job that paid a lot more than GE, but it was operating a jack hammer on a construction job, which wasn't what I intended to do for a living. So, I worked on that job until the weather got cold. I called GE and asked to start work while I was waiting for my clearance. So now I was a GE employee. My badge # was 2118, which meant I was employee number 2,118 on the top-secret ANDP program. This area was called the "P" area. There wasn't anything to do but wait there until GE got all the security info. The security clearance was called "Q" clearance. Everyone who got to work on the ANPD project required a "Q" clearance. This was the most important clearance in the United States. It was because of the nuclear work.

We told stories, played cards, just to pass the time of day. The average time to wait for all the security background investigation was around three months. It took me longer than anyone else. I don't know why, but it took me thirteen months to get my top-secret clearance. All the information I had from the lab where I would be working was I'd be making strain gages. What could I be doing? So, with nothing to do, I got everything I could find about strain gages. After all the research, I wrote a paper on the history of the strain gage. I found a lot of the information about the strain gage from the engineers in the "P" area who were just waiting for their "Q" clearance. GE found it interesting and provided me with books so I could study about the strain gage. I eventually got my "Q" clearance and went to the strain-gage lab. I knew more about this little wire strain gage than most of the technicians who were making them.

P. Allan Hill worked on the top-secret multiple independently targeted reentry vehicle (MIRV) that carried thirteen nuclear weapons on board the minute man missile system into space.

P. A. HILL is a Mechanical Specialist in Experimental Structural Mechanics responsible for supporting the photoelastic activities of the laboratory and planning, developing and conducting experimental programs. He has been directly involved with the evaluation of structures and structural components and problems in shock absorption, high pressure explosive effects, heat transfer, ground support equipment, crack propagation studies and deep submergence vessel instrumentation. He was a Mechanical Systems Test Conductor, responsible for conducting tests in accordance with prepared test plans for design assessment and compatibility checks of subsystem and ground service equipment.

Mr. Hill received training as a Horologist from Western Penn Horological Institute and the USAF and completed Mechanical Engineering Courses at the University of Cincinnati.

He worked with techniques for high temperature strain gages, complex thermocouple installations and printed circuitry on brittle materials at the Aircraft Nuclear Propulsion Department of General Electric and was associated with pioneering activities in the industrial use of photoelastic reflection techniques.

GENERAL ⊕ ELECTRIC
Re-entry & Environmental Systems Division
3198 Chestnut St., Philadelphia, Pa. 19101

COPIES: AM Garber
RT Mayer
NH Blumstein
JC Truscott
Dr. AL Ross
HL Debes
HW Breiling
JA Fedorochko
Personnel File

SUBJECT:

RESEARCH & ENGINEERING DRIVE AWARD
FIRST PLACE WINNER – MAY
CRAFTSMANSHIP

June 28, 1971

Mr. Alan Hill
Room 8426–U VF

It gives me great personal pleasure to express to you, on behalf of the management of Research and Engineering, congratulations on your outstanding work in obtaining residual stress test measurements in a short time period, assuring customer satisfaction was achieved and production schedules were met for the vehicles.

We are proud to have men of your ability in Research and Engineering; and it is my pleasure to present you with the Research and Engineering First Place Craftsmanship Award for the month of May, 1971, DRIVE in token recognition of your performance.

Dr. J. D. Stewart, General Manager
Research and Engineering Department

JDS/JAF/meg

Strain-Gage History: 1954

I WAS VERY interested in what I was going to be doing at this new job at GE—making strain gages in the strain-gage lab. What is a strain gage? I've got nothing to do while waiting for my top-secret "Q" clearance, which will take approximately six or eight months, so I'll see what I can learn about the strain gage. The strain gage had been around only for ten or twelve years. I started asking questions that helped me develop an understanding of the applications for strain gages at GE.

There were about 150 employees winding strain gages. Most of the gages were made for the GE Jet Engine Department, which was separate from the ANPD. The employees at the ANPD were called the Ivy league crew. With our "Q" clearance we could go anywhere in the company. The strain-gage lab at the ANPD had about fifty watchmakers. We were told the production was an average of two gages per person per day. They could make more than that, but only two would meet the resistance tolerance of two ohms per strain gage. Maybe the money wasn't great, but I felt like a lucky boy to have a such a wonderful job. To become a strain-gage winder, I had to practice one year before I could be in the production department.

I was the only person who would be working with strain gages. I found all the information that was available to me. In 1938, the US government asked MIT to learn more about stress, especially the stress that was applied to a water tower during the earthquake in the early 1900s in California. I next found the man who would build the model of the water tower. He was from Clarksburg, West Virginia, and his name was Frank Hines. In 1932, General Motors Company offered a four-year education at MIT to the person who could make a perfect model of the Napoleon's Wedding Coach. Mr. Hines would be the man to build a model of the water tower to be tested. The tower had to be vibrated from the records of the 1920 Long Beach California earthquake and Professor Ruge was a PhD and was going to conduct the test. He wanted to measure the dynamic strain on the tower. Professor Ruge saw a solution to the strain measurement problem, which required a fine insulated wire. Professor Ruge's tests were not what he had expected, but a patent was applied for by Professor Ruge. In 1938, Ed Simmons, an electrical engineer working for Hugh's Tool Company, wanted to know the stress applied to a drill shaft while drilling. He used Professor Ruge's fine wire method, but Mr. Simmons came up with equipment that could measure the stress so it could be used as a gage.

In 1940, the Baldwin Locomotive Company needed a gage for measuring stress on locomotive parts. Frank Tatnall, the head engineer of Baldwin, hired a Baldwin patent attorney to lay the legal groundwork for a joint interest of the two strain-gage inventors who almost simultaneously and independently for two different purposes, invented the strain gage. Frank Tatnall said, "What will we call this tiny wire thing?" We needed a name to get it registered with a trademark. We had Mr. Simmons, Professor Ruge and his right-hand man, and myself. We'll call it "S" for Simmons, "R" for Ruge, and there were four of us at this table. It was decided we would call it (S-R-4) gage. Now, sixty years later, the wire strain gage is called S-R-4 gage by the old timers.

The strain gage was secured to the material to be tested with Ducoâ cement (household cement). The structure was subjected to a force it minutely to stretch the wire filament changing its electrical resistance to a current flow, or impedance, as measured in ohms. When strain or force is applied, the resistance changes and is displayed on an ohmmeter. Scaling will permit reading directly by the strain in the part, or force applied.

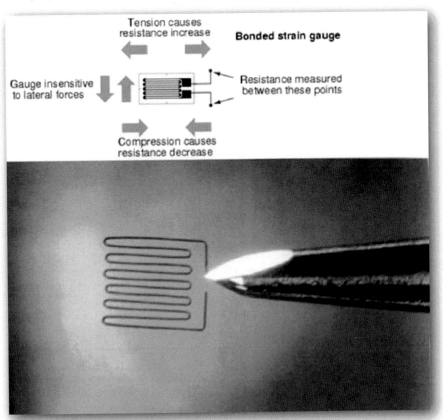

P. Allan Hill's wire wound strain gage is incredibly small. Shown on the end of a fine jewelers' tweezer, the strain gage's wire diameter is 0.0008 inch or 0.26 the diameter or one-fourth the diameter of a human hair. Allan made thousands of strain gages!

During World War II the aircraft industry in Los Angeles, California, put the strain gage on the map. It's literally true that the modern high-performance aircraft would not be possible if not for the strain gage. For the first time designs were being made based on actual tests under simulated flights conditions on the ground. In the prototype aircraft, fuselage would be plastered with thousands of gages, monitoring strain at critical parts of the fuselage, as dozens of hydraulic jacks applied loads to the aircraft structure, programmed to simulate flight.

In 1954, there was another type of strain gage developed. The S-R-4 gage is a wire gage, depending on the type of wire the gage is made of. The temperature can be as high as 2,000 degrees Fahrenheit for a short time. The new gage is called foil gage. I'm not sure how its produced, but it's much better than the wire gage but it's only good to withstand 540 degrees Fahrenheit.

So, while working in the strain-gage lab, I'll be working with the wire gage because the nuclear reaction gets very hot. Because of the nuclear work, I wasn't cleared to know anything other than what I needed for making gages. From what information I could get, it surely did sound interesting.

The Baldwin Company had about fifty girls at well-lighted, microscope-equipped tables, painstakingly winding one mill (0.0001") wire around groups of pins on a jig you could hold in your hand. A piece of paper below the wire, Duco â cement, and a piece of paper on top of the wire completed the sandwich. The gage length was short as 1/16" to 1/8" and finding people with the training, skill, and patience to become a good gage winder was difficult. The demand for the aircraft company was so great the delivery of a package of five gages took sixty to ninety days. I was really interested in wire strain gages, but no one could talk to me about the gages. I'll have to practice making gages for one year before they would be expected to be used.

There were about sixty to eighty people with a "P" clearance waiting for their "Q" clearance. I was the only one going into the strain-gage lab, so I didn't talk much with others. I felt most of them were too educated to for my type of work, so I did all my research on my own and the history of the S-R-4 gage was what I learned.

From that point on, I was a part of making history and was a pioneer in the field of strain gages. Allan Hill making history was something I could not believe! While at GE and after GE, I was motivated to continue my work in the field of strain gages and I founded a new company: Strain-O-Therm Technology, Inc. The wire gage has been my livelihood for over sixty years and life couldn't have been any better.

I had no idea at the time that in the 1980s Strain-O-Therm Technology, Inc. was the supplier of wire strain gages to every company that makes a jet engine in the free world. Imagine that!

I sure did love my job, but at home there were things that had to be taken care of, so I had to focus on that. Lila and I moved into an apartment where there were maybe two hundred families. We couldn't afford much. We had a couch that could be made up into a bed, and that was it. We needed a table and chairs, but we couldn't go to Sears and get something and charge it like you do now. We had to eat on the floor for a few weeks until we could buy something.

I've been so lucky about having a wife who can make do when things are difficult. Hutchie Lee started taking care of my money, and it's been that way for sixty-five years. Now we don't have to worry anymore. Lila Lee took a bunch of envelopes, marked one rent, one food, one savings, and one for church. We tried to meet these each month. Hutchie Lee said she would like to buy some Christmas gifts for the family, but how can we afford anything. I made enough money to keep Hutchie happy with Christmas gifts. We could now afford to make the trip back home for Christmas.

While at home I packed my watch tools so that I could do some watch repair. Things seemed to be as good as life can be. Just think, I'm now working at the world's most important job, and at the great company GE. What have I done to deserve this great work? I felt I was doing fine winding gages. We had an engineer. I never knew his background other than that he was about seventy some years old, was a PhD who retired from Bell Labs, and was now with GE. He wasn't a GE employee, but something like a contractor and a wonderful man to work for. He told me I was doing a good job, which I tried very hard to do my best.

About six months into my year of practice, I asked Mr. Kurts, who was my supervisor, "Why don't you have a machine to make these strain gages?" His responded saying, "No one can make a machine that will do that."

As far as I could tell there were only two employees who had horological training and I was one of them. When I told Mr. Kurts, "I think I could think of a way to make a machine to wind gages" he said, "If you think you can come up with a machine, I'll make an area for you to work in." Now here I was having no idea what I was going to do, but I was expected to come up with something.

Day after day, for three months, I thought of a method to automate strain-gage production. I made some sketches of my idea, and Mr. Kurts sent my sketches to the drafting department and oddly claimed it was his idea and he should get the US patent. However, GE knew the invention was my idea and I got the US patent. I got one hundred dollars as a share of GE stock, and the machine belonged to GE Company.

All this time I was dreaming. "Will this idea work?" It's got to work as my future at GE will depend on its success. No one will ever know how many hours I spent at night thinking about how to make this machine. This was a time I realized how bad I needed drafting ability. All I know now was how to make a sketch describing my plans. With the drawings from the drafting department, the plans were sent to a machine company in North Ohio to be built. This took two or three months.

With my watch tools set up in the apartment, I must get some homework to do. One day a new employee asked me to repair his watch. I'd never seen this employee before. All I knew was he came from Goodyear Atomic Department. I repaired his watch and I never saw him again. His name was Jack Parker, so I'll tell more about him eight years from now.

Now you can't believe how important this strain-gage winding machine was to the GE company. My plans were to make it as simple as possible, so anyone could make a gage. All you had to do was put a spool of wire in the machine, pull a handle, and the gage would come out. The same gage, having same gage resistance each time. The machine was delivered to the strain-gage lab. Everyone wanted to see this very important tool for the strain-gage lab. Dr. Shoults was there to see this thing make a gage. It looked fine to me. I put a spool of wire in place, pulled the handle, and a gage come out. But it wasn't the size GE wanted. My heart stopped when I saw this odd gage. The first thing I did was look at the problem and it was plain for me to see.

Meanwhile Dr. Shoults asked me, "Why did you design a machine that wouldn't work?" I saw the problem as soon as I looked at the machine. I had asked for the small thin arms to be 0.010 inches thick with pins to wrap the wire around. The pins were supposed to be 0.005 inches in diameter in my sketch, which I sent to the drafting department. No one would admit how the changes were made. My original sketch indicated that I had wanted the arms to be 0.010 inches thick and indicated pins that were 0.005 inches in diameter. I showed my original sketch to the draftsman and this fixed the problem.

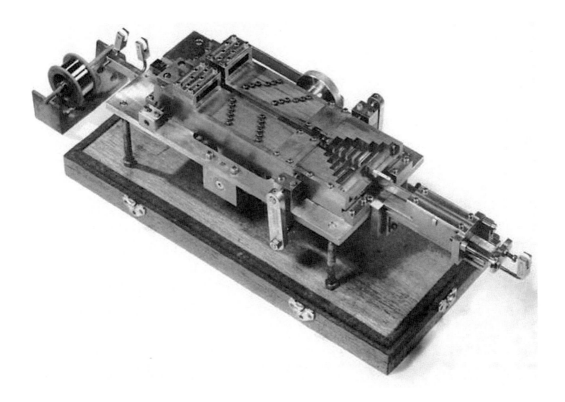

This is the prototype of my invention of the original semiautomated wire wound strain-gage machine. This was my first US patent, and for this invention GE compensated me with one hundred dollars in shares of GE stock. Unfortunately, the US patent and the machine belonged to GE. Years later, when the patent protection expired, I would make many improvements and build my business Strain-O-Therm, Inc. around this semiautomated wire wound strain-gage production technology.

For a moment, I thought my job at GE was over, but the problem turned out to be one of the first wonderful blessings I've had. When I showed Dr. Shoults why it didn't work, I received a prestigious job title of "Individual Contributor" and my life at GE changed forever.

By the way the strain-gage production machine cost $48,000 in 1955 ($436,300 in 2017) and the machine design was made to my drawings but not to the size my sketches required. The only answer was that GE couldn't rebuild it to my incredibly small requirement. I never knew who said it couldn't be done, but Dr. Shoults came back to the lab one afternoon asked why I designed the machine the way I did. I showed him why I designed the machine the way I did. I found an arm 0.007 thick much smaller than the 0.010 thick arm GE used, and I got a 0.003 pin and placed in the hole in the arm. Dr. Shoults looked at the parts and thought for a minute and said, "I didn't know that could be done!" He said to my boss, "I don't want this man making strain gages. He's going to work on the Fuel Cell project." By the way, I still have that small arm in a special box now sixty years later. I don't know who was responsible for that mistake, but it changed my life for the best.

I spent the rest of my eighteen years of employment at GE with the job title of "Individual Contributor." As an Individual Contributor, my first job was to investigate measuring the forces to detect a break in a piece of material. This part was a fuel tube made of ceramic, something like glass mixed with 4238, a material that I think it is still classified, so I won't explain any further. The test specimen was 8" long with a note 0.3" in diameter. I was told to paint a circuit inside the tube. The circuit had to be a material that would stand 2,000 degrees Fahrenheit. It couldn't be more than 0.001 inches thick. This was a very important job; the fuel element was cracking and the engineers wanted to know when it was happening. When the tube would crack while at high temperatures, engineers would detect a crack when the circuit was broken. What I had in mind was I'd get to the chemistry lab to make the conductive material, which would stand 2,000 degrees Fahrenheit. I'd paint two straight lines of conductive material down through the tube. I made two long tubes to hold the conductive material and hook the tubes to two large syringes and make a pusher to push the syringes down. This was easy. I'd just pull the tube through the small metal tubes with the conductive material. Now there was a question. I was concerned if the tube to be tested would crack when the conductive circuit wouldn't detect the crack. I had to paint the circuit around inside the tube, which, of course, was another big problem. I had to design a procedure to paint the circuit around the inside of the tube. As I walked by the machine shop, I saw a wheel handle for turning a part of a lathe. I was going to have to turn the tube as it's painted. So I'll go to the machine shop, have them make a shaft with threads to the pitch I'll paint the inside of the tube while I was turning the tube. Now I've got to make a holder for the tube at the end of the shaft while it's being rotated. Now this is one of the most important projects, because it's a very serious problem. I had got permission to go to any department and get what I wanted to get done, right away. Now I've got the conductive material. I've got the syringes and this small nine-inch-long tubes to hold the conductor while I'm turning the handle swirling the painted conductive material inside the tube that's being painted. I had to make some of the parts myself. The small tubes that carried the conductive material, the little motors that pushed the syringes, and the pin vice parts that were attached to the end of the shaft to hold the part that I was painting. As the tube was filled with conductive material, they were placed completely through the tube to be painted. I started to push the material through the syringes and out of the small tubes. Then I started turning the handle and the tube was painted inside as I turned the handle, and when the conductive material came out of the other end of the part that was being painted, I had painted the circuit, but now I must paint one end of the tube when the circuit starts to connect the two painted circuits so I can have full circuit, which will show if you have a crack anywhere in the fuel tube. This project was completed and successful tests were completed in ten days. They only part I had some other department to do was the shaft.

I was given another very important job working on a nuclear fuel element. I never did understand anything about the nuclear field, but knew I had to be careful. There were five-inch material cans, about five inches high and about four inches in diameter for the largest one. The next one was smaller. There was a gap of 0.010 inch between each can. The cans were filled with uranium-238 so you had to be careful.

The problem was GE wanted to know what the temperature was between each of the uranium-238 filled cans. GE wanted to know what the temperature is half way down or at 2.5". The diameter was approximately 0.010 of an inch or 10 mils or three times the thickness of a human hair, and it was inconceivable to locate a thermocouple in a tube that small. Now no one could tell me, just we don't know how, and we need the temperature at that point. I didn't know anything about thermocouples at this point. I found that a thermocouple must have two different materials. During testing the high temperature would approach 2,000 degrees Fahrenheit! This would require 90 percent platinum and 10 percent rhodium. The cans were 0.010 apart so the thermocouple must be small as 0.010 dia. Now the thermocouple wire must be insulated and I was not getting any help on this project. There isn't any way you can find an insulated thermocouple that small. So, I got some platinum 0.003 inches in diameter without the insulation, and had to improvise on how to insulate the wire. No one at GE could help me. I found a piece of quartz tubing with a hole about 0.030 in diameter. With this if it can be heated hot enough, I can pull it down to the size of 0.010 inches and I can use it for insulation. Now I was not sure of anything. I was just sure they want to know the temperature inside, or between each can. This seemed to be the only thing I can do. After so many failures pulling the quartz to size, I was about to give up. I got a tube of quartz 0.010 that would fit between the cans. I pushed the 0.003 diameter wire into the small hole. Now this requires two wires for a thermocouple, so I welded the platinum and the plat 10 percent R. The end-to-end polish was welded bead down small enough to go into the quartz tube. One end of the thermocouple went out of the bottom and the other the top. The junction of the couple was at the 2.5" between the cans. I had solved the problem.

P. Allan Hill improvised using syringes paint an electrical circuit for a thermocouple to measure temperatures up to 2,000° F inside a tube of uranium-238 for the GE top-secret Aircraft Nuclear Propulsion Department (ANDP) program. Mr. Hill developed this machine using a rotating tool to paint a conductive material inside the tube. The diameter of the tube above is approximately 0.010 of an inch or 10 mils or three times the thickness of a human hair, and it was inconceivable to locate a thermocouple in a tube that small. P. Allan Hill found a way!

This was a job that was spent in many sleepless nights wondering what the next day will be like. I can't say I didn't like that kind of work. I really loved it. I've always liked to work alone, and at this very important job I had all the help I needed. Like the quartz insulation, I didn't know what quartz was, or what a thermocouple was. All I had to do was ask for help, and I got lots of it, but I had to know how to use it. If someone else knew how to do what I was asked to do, they would have done it. Anyway, I got to feeling important when I could go to any GE department and ask for help, and I got it quickly because this was a special problem with the fuel elements.

My work at GE in many ways was what I wanted to do.

Many things needed to be developed and tested. I started painting circuits on ceramic material. I was testing new materials that could be used for fuel elements. I did almost anything I wanted to do. I'd tell my supervisor what I had in mind for my next project and most always he'd say OK. Sometimes they had other problems to work on.

Strain gages were always on my mind.

When a gage is made, it is held in place with a piece of tape while removing it from the handheld winding device. Then the gages are taped onto a glass medical slide. This is the way the strain gage is inventoried and stored until it's needed. The tape has a shelf life and if it wasn't used for a few weeks the gage is of no use. This was a problem that I solved. I decided to flatten the gage, so it will hold its shape. The gage, when taken off the winding fixture without the tape holding its shape, was like a spring and would spread apart. I can see I'll have to have the machine shop take a hand steel block cut a slot in the block approximately 0.0005 inches deep. The wire that is used for strain gages is 0.0008 inches in diameter. Maybe I can lay a flat block on top of the gage now in the slot and press it flat to see how it works. Many hours went into making it work.

Each time I did something, it showed enough progress to make another test necessary to try something else. First, I had the machine shop cut the slot in the one block, which I used for pressing. I first make a gage and then cut a piece a tape to hold the gage shape while removing the gage. Then I had the chemistry lab to make a soft adhesive, just hard enough to hold the gage down in the slot in the bottom block. Then with the gage held in place with the adhesive, I'll remove the tape. Now this was a difficult job. Everything was going perfect until I'd pull the tape off the gage. When I did, the tape was so sticky that it would pull the gage off the block. The adhesive wouldn't hold the gage down on the block. I tried a new type of tape, a plain old scotch tape. It was much better than the masking tape, but sometimes it would pull the gage away from the block. I had to have something that worked all the time. I took the scotch tape, took a pair of jeweler's tweezers, and pulled the piece of scotch tape through my fingers, removing some of the sticky material from the tape. Now the tape had just enough adhesive to hold the gage in place while applying the cement adhesive. I delicately pulled the tape away from the top of the gage and then waited for the top block to be placed and applied pressure. After a few tries finding just the right pressure, now we had a perfect flattened gage looking like it did when it was made. A development like this doesn't happen overnight; it takes hours and weeks working on this and that and mostly that. No one could have loved the work I was doing like I could, and something good was coming from it.

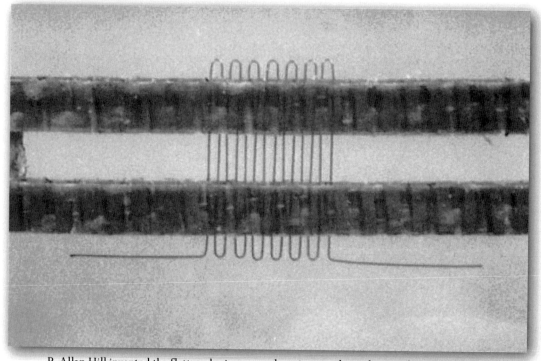

P. Allan Hill invented the flattened wire—wound strain gage shown here under transfer tape.
The gage's wire diameter is 0.0008 inch or 0.26 the diameter or one-quarter the diameter of a human hair.
Allan made thousands of strain gages!

The flattened strain gage was my invention. This was an engineering breakthrough for the GE Jet Engine Department, as well as the GE aircraft nuclear propulsion department. I know the flattened gage wasn't as important as the fuel element problems, but it was very important for the GE gage department. The last few weeks were spent working with strain gages. There was a big problem with the high-temperature adhesive used to apply the strain gage onto the structure to be tested. The strain gages made by the strain-gage lab were called the "wire gage" and was used for high temperature or hostile environments.

When I first started at GE in 1954, most strain gages used were of the wire gage type. By about 1955 there was another gage called the foil gage in use. The foil gage was 100 percent better to work with because it produces better information than the wire gage, but the foil gage wasn't functional at temperatures greater than about 550 degrees Fahrenheit. The foil had the name of "lick them-stick them." The first foil gages I used were applied to the specimen to be tested with Duco cement.

One day a salesman came to our lab and showed me a new gage product. There were eight or ten of us waiting to see what he has. He said, "Boys hold your hands out and I'm going to put a drop of my product on your fingers. Hold your fingers tight for one minute." Would you believe that we couldn't get our fingers apart until we cut them apart? That was our introduction to super glue!

The salesman's name was Bill Bean, a well-known authority on the foil strain gages. My interest was still with the use of wire gage. I found my time, almost full time testing different adhesives for the use of wire gage. I found products that were wonderful at temperatures less than 1,000 degrees Fahrenheit. I was testing the different materials and found one that was just what we needed for higher temperature tests on the material to be tested. I got word that another lab was also doing some testing of ways to apply the gage to the specimen to be tested.

I was watching the gage being applied with the new technology. It looked to me like taking a high-temperature torch and applying some sort of power on the gage. I thought I'd better continue with my work for developing a good adhesive. The torch will damage more gages than the gage lab can make. So, I continued my work with the new adhesive I'd found. This is something I had a hard time believing. The superglue adhesive I'd found couldn't be ordered because the company that produced it made a mistake in the formula and they don't know how they made it. That was the end of my adhesive research. I thought, "Let them burn up the gages with a torch. It'll make the gage more profitable someday." My way was completely off because all wire gages are applied using what it called as the flame spray technique. This process results in many damaged gages, but the flame spray is good to 2,000 degrees Fahrenheit testing.

I had a lot of contacts with the many PhD engineers I worked with and they always questioned me on why I did not get my college degree. All I knew was the mechanics of making things work. What a blessing the school of horology was to me. Nothing else would have been to my liking as the school.

Now, I need to learn some engineering.

The ANPD had the best engineers in the United States. One of my best friends was Ed Aitken, a PhD and a nuclear engineer from California. We were such good friends and our wives were good friends. Ed had just got his PhD and his first job was with GE. The Korean War had just ended and Ed was afraid he might be drafted into the service and he didn't want to invest in a car so they used our car until he could afford one and felt free of being drafted into the service. Ed did his best to teach me something and he didn't know where to start.

Our daughter, Lila Jane, was born in 1956 and I remember how I'd take her down to the wash room, hold her in one arm and a book in the other. It seems for a few years all I did was study.

In 1957, I had the opportunity to meet Nina Ramsey and Nokey, who were engineers from Turkey. They both came to the United States to get their master's education in chemical engineering. They got their master's from Florida University. Nina got pregnant and this made it possible for them to stay in the United States after the baby was born. Ramsey went to Northwestern University and got his PhD. So, Nina thought if Hutchie and I would come over to talk to Ramsey, he would feel better talking to someone away from work, because he had difficulty with English. Ramsey was a very lovely person, and he liked me and I liked him. He said, "Why don't I teach you and go to college?"

After about two years of Ramsey's teaching, he felt I was ready to take a test at Cincinnati University, one of best engineering schools in the United States. I took my first class in Algebra and received an "A." Boy, I thought I was on top of the world. The hardest work I ever did was learning to study. I had so much to learn.

So many things in life I'll never understand.

Keep trying, and do whatever you do the best that can be done.

I also feel that when you do good things, blessings just show up from nowhere and make your most wonderful life just a whole lot better.

After thinking about my odd and unusual life, I know that I was born to be blessed.

I felt I could do anything that could be done.

All I needed was a chance to try.

Some of the college professors from schools like MIT come to study some of the things we were doing for the first time. Most of these teachers didn't have a "Q" clearance and I would guide them to some of the places they wanted to see that wasn't in the "Q" area. One teacher from Purdue University in Indiana took a liking to me and asked if I would go back to Purdue and be his assistant in his school lab. I didn't want to leave GE, but it made me feel good that someone away from GE liked what I could do.

Now, I was going to school every night and the one class I needed and liked best was mechanical drawing. The teacher said, "I don't give an A grade because that would mean a perfect drawing and I haven't seen one." So, my desire was to make a B. I took two years of mechanical drawing and I made a B each year.

I got into some deep math and I never did understand what I needed to know to be an engineer. I was lucky to receive college credit for many career experiences that I had so far in my life. I received credit for my time in the US Navy, my horological school, and my time in the US Air Force, and the work I was doing at GE.

So, I didn't have to finish college to become an engineer. All I had to do was to take a test for PE (professional engineer) and you had a title engineer at GE. I had the pay rate as high as I could get without my PE.

I got to thinking about my background and how far I had come. Dad wasn't a good father, but he taught me things other young boys had no chance to learn. I had no love, but from Dad I did learn a lot about important things in life. Dad said over and over, education isn't important you have to learn to "work hard and be honest." He said, "Be to work on time. If you get paid for eight hours give eight hours. Don't be late for work; it won't hurt to be there a few minutes early." Dad was in the construction cement and wall building business and he always said, "The most important thing about buildings is the foundation, and be sure to make the foundation strong, so the wall will not fall."

I've always done all these things even though there wasn't love from Dad and it was those tough lessons that not many young boys ever learn. I'm now going to work on the most important job in the world and looking back I can thank Dad. Education is important, very important, but some of the things Dad taught me are also important.

Life at GE was like a great big playground for me. I was feeling great and it was time for me to trade cars. My old Studebaker was eight years old. Things were going better than I'd ever dreamed. I'm now working on watches for a large jewelry store in Cincinnati. I was specializing on chronographs special stop watches. The pay was good, and I wanted a car that would last longer than ten years. The Studebaker shop also sold Mercedes Benz cars. The diesel Mercedes caught my eye. The salesman told me that model Mercedes is what they use in Germany for taxi cabs and some have gone over 100,000 miles. In June 1959, I ordered a Mercedes. It was delivered on December 17, 1959, but technically a 1960 model. It was the first diesel in Cincinnati, Ohio. Well, not the first because some service men had brought Mercedes back from Germany, but my car was made for the US market. The car wasn't what I ordered. I ordered the car with a front set to be a straight bench seat because we now had a baby two months old and I needed the bench set to hold the baby seat. To get another car would take a year, so I took the one they sent. The price of that car was $3,778 as compared to $2,000 for a new Cadillac at that time. I've still got it now in 2017. Last year I had the car inspection and the shop noted I had only driven the car sixteen miles this year. I now have over 250,000 miles on the car!

MISSILE AND

SPACE DIVISION

VALLEY FORGE SPACE TECHNOLOGY CENTER (MAIL: P. O. BOX 8555, PHILA. 1, PA.) . . . TEL. 969-2000

SPACECRAFT
DEPARTMENT

November 14, 1963

TO WHOM IT MAY CONCERN:

This letter will help introduce Mr. "Al" Hill to you.

During the course of the past year, it has been my pleasure to have had
"Al's" assistance on a variety of projects ranging from moving a large and
extremely delicate structure into a limited space, to designing and building
several gadgets to improve equipment operation. "Al" brings to each task,
no matter how large or how small, the same air of courtesy, quiet efficiency,
preparation as required, know-how and ability to follow through. When the
seemingly impossible job of moving the large structure was given to Al, he
immediately began locating all the drawings he needed; he studied them and
made layouts which showed some two inches to spare. Solely on the basis
of "Al's" prediction the structure was brought in; the sketches proved
correct, the clearance was of the order of two inches and the task was
successfully completed.

"Al" has also proved himself an accomplished gadgeteer in his work to improve
operation of the bifilar pendulum. He designed and built, completely without
supervision, a centering and release device to aid in imparting pure rotational
motion to the pendulum.

"Al" needs only the definition of the job. He goes ahead and gets it done.
I know that I speak for the many people with whom "Al" has come into contact
here when I say that his manner and his abilities have won him much respect.

S. Rodkin, Environmental Test Engineer
Nimit Systems Evaluation Engineering
Room U2407, Ext. 4042

NASA and the Lunar Excursion Module (LEM)

An astronaut works outside the Lunar Landing Module on the moon.

I LIKED MY next job, which was material testing for the Lunar Landing Module Insulation Tiles.

It is important that the reader realizes that all my work up until this time was without the aid of digital computers. The Lunar Landing Module Insulation Tiles required a lot of testing and this is what I wanted to do. The project was a classified material that was approximately 1" × 1" × 12" long. I got the new job because of my strain-gage work at ANPD in Cincinnati, Ohio. This twelve-inch beam was secured in a base, which would hold it when we tested it. A small explosive was detonated at the end of the beam, and a strain gage secured onto the beam so that we could measure the strain on the beam when strained by a detonation wave front from an explosive detonating. The explosive work had to be done in a special facility forty miles west of the Valley Forge Space Center. The town where the testing took place was Morgantown, Pennsylvania. There was an Amish Farmer who had a stone quarry, which was about three hundred feet deep and it was dry and this was the quarry that GE used for explosive work.

GE had a lot of explosive testing at Morgantown, Pennsylvania. I was assigned to support an odd old engineer, a man I will call "Mr. X," whom I'd never seen before. He didn't think much of me, and I didn't do a lot to change his mind. We could have completed ten or twelve tests a day, but the engineer wanted to complete only one test and then go back to the space center. "Mr. X" wouldn't sit in the passenger car seat and he only sat in the back seat. We did one test a day for about six weeks and after each test, something happened. We had no data, and worse yet, the test was a complete failure. One day while driving back to the space center, Mr. X said to me, "I've been observing the test, and you and Dr. Howard Seeman were the last people out of the test bunker, and I want you to watch, keep an eye on Dr. Seeman, because I think he is sabotaging our tests." I only thought Mr. X was just making small talk because Dr. Seeman was the last person you would think would harm anybody or anything. I laughed it off as a joke. The next day after we had another failed test. Mr. X said to me while driving to the space center, "Remember I told you Dr. Seeman was sabotaging our test; well today you were the last person out of the bunker, and I think you are sabotaging our tests!" We were on the Pennsylvania turnpike, and I stopped the car demanded he get out, but he refused to get out of the back seat! When I got to the office, I went to the office and told our manager, "I'll never work with Mr. X again." My manager knew that Mr. X was an odd person and wanted me to continue the testing because we needed the data. I knew I needed to understand why the tests were failing, and first checked the power source and the firing cable and found there was a break in the insulation. I found a microscope, took one inch apart, and found small pieces of shrapnel had cut the cable wire. No problem. I'd get a conduit, pipe to put the cable in, and it would now be protected. Two days later we could test with no problems, and Dr. Seeman helped me get the data we needed to complete the testing.

Mr. X got sick at work and wanted to go to the hospital in downtown Philadelphia, Pennsylvania. Mr. X had a VW car and wanted me to take him to the hospital, and after all our troubles, I was the only person he knew who would help him. I took him to the hospital. I don't remember how I got back home, but he died at the hospital with a disease of the brain.

My next project involved a Hercules Aerospace product made of boron, which Hercules thought GE could use for jet engine after-burner business. GE wanted the material and wanted to test to see if it was as good as the Hercules product. Hercules represented that the material had already been tested, but GE required test validation. The Hercules engineer with the program was Dick Ravenhall, who suggested we both test the material together.

We went to the old Baldwin locomotive plant outside Pennsylvania. They had all the testing equipment necessary for testing. I oversaw the testing. Dick Ravenhall, the Hercules engineer, and I didn't agree on several things. We got the tests finished. Everyone was happy except Mr. Ravenhall, who was concerned because Hercules was closing the plant, where Mr. Ravenhall was the top dog. He was now transferred to Hercules plant at Cumberland, Maryland.

Mr. Ravenhall was offered a position at GE Space Center, but he wanted to stay with Hercules. It should be noted that Dick became the best friend I ever had. Dick and his wife put their home in Levittown, Pennsylvania, on the market to sell. Dick drove to Maryland and wrote a check for the down payment on a house there. Dick and his wife both grew up in New York City. On the way home from Maryland, his wife Hilda cried all the way home and said, "I don't want to live in the mountains." So, Dick took his home off the market, canceled his check on the home in Maryland, and took the job at GE.

GE set up a new program called structure lab, which Dick would oversee and I would support him in the testing. Dick will now be my boss; we hadn't agreed on much while we were testing at Baldwin. Although I was happy that I'd be back in a lab testing, I wasn't sure about Dick Ravenhall. This was a new program with a testing lab. Dick will have an office far away from the lab. I'll be in the lab, and we'll have three technicians. I'll oversee the lab.

The Orbiting Astrological

Observatory

In 1968, I was assigned to the Orbiting Astrological Observatory (OAO) project to work on a problem balancing the spacecraft. The OAO space vehicle was an early space observatory and led the way for the Hubble Space Observatory.

The OAO was approximately two tons of steel sitting in a dish of air under pressure. It was so well balanced that you could move the two-ton spacecraft with a very light touch. The instability problem occurred on operating the "star tracker," which caused the vehicle to become unbalanced. After a few weeks with no answer as to why this happened, Mr. Page, a GE vice president, called Lou Gattesndamner, who was GE's best troubleshooter, to come and look at our problem. Lou was busy with a problem in South Africa and would come to help us after his next job. I was told I'd be his assistant when he arrived. He would be in complete control of whatever needed to be done. The first thing Lou wanted was to stop all work on the OAO at 5:00 p.m. until 8:00 a.m. the next morning. Lou and I looked at every problem that could be a problem. Lou would go see Mr. Page after 8:00 a.m. and report on problems and our progress. We worked all night sometimes and we didn't take a break all night. I told Lou I wish I was rich so I could go work with him every day the rest of my life. I could see why he was GE's number one troubleshooter. He would look at problems differently, and he solved the problem.

When in outer space, this OAO spacecraft would look at a star, lock onto it with "star trackers" and then another "star tracker" 120 degrees on the side of the spacecraft would lock onto it. Then the craft would look for another star 120 degrees and lock onto it. The scientist's study what stars the OAO locks onto, so the camera would see what the scientist wanted to look at. Our problem was that the spacecraft's little thrusters or jets would move the OAO spacecraft around. Then the OAO would lock onto the star they had preplanned. Then the OAO spacecraft would move the "star tracker" around and then lock onto the other preplanned star.

Now with the three "star trackers" locked on, the OAO camera is looking at the heavenly body the scientist wants to see. Our problem was we could use the jets to move the craft so the "star trackers" would lock the craft in place. Two or three seconds later, the craft would become unbalanced and fall over. I asked myself why this was happening? This was a problem and we solved it. Lou found the problem to be in the IBM electric control package. Now this is before all the electronic gadgets, chips, and digital components we have today. Lou found the wiring in the package got hot and caused the craft to become unbalanced. Now how do we solve the problem? We solved the problem, believe it or not, with a strain gage. There isn't any way I could explain how we solved the problem.

Deep Sea Bed Oil Drilling: Project Bottom Fix

———— ❦ ————

I WAS BACK with my old friend Dick Ravenhall. Dick has an idea of drilling for oil on the ocean floor. It was called Bottom Fix. Bottom Fix was a General Electric Company Missile and Space Division project developed for deep-sea-bed oil drilling systems capabilities. Dick thought this could be possible. We made a model about twenty feet in diameter. This was one of the more interesting tests. The framework of the model is titanium material. The windows are made of a material from Corning Glass Company. This model had to withstand extreme hydrostatic pressures at the bottom of the ocean to the depths of twenty thousand feet. The material and sealants must be designed to seal between the metal and glass window. The first test required a gasket seal made of a thin gold strip. The thought was the gold is soft and it'll make a good seal. The glass material was a 5/8" thick. I cut a piece 5/8" × 5/8" and designed a test to simulate very high pressure, and this test was something no one at GE ever saw before. The cube could be pressured down from 5/8" down to 1/2" and the material would not encounter fatigue. This material was resilient and withstood the fatigue, unlike a nail, which after bending ten times or so will undergo fatigue and break. This material and glass would be good for the undersea windows. When pressure is applied on the unit, the more the pressure the tighter it become and made a good seal.

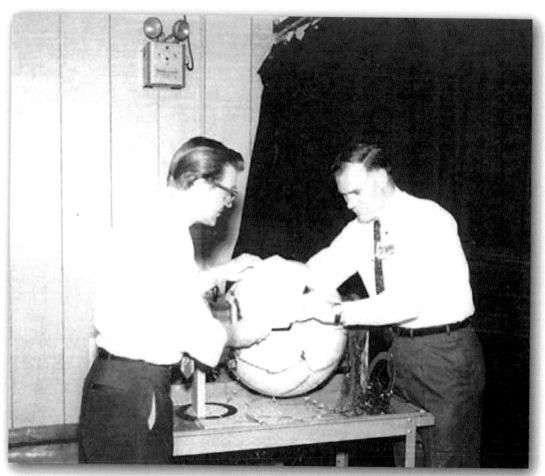

P. Allan Hill (on right) working on a test specimen for Project Bottom Fix.

Dick Ravenhall: "An Engineer's Engineer"

———— ❧ ————

THE NEXT THING I worked on was with my friend Dick Ravenhall. Dick and I worked on all these other problems together, but sometimes I'd go off and work alone, but Dick was always my boss. Dick was not only my boss but we loved working together. The engineers would think of anything that might be a good idea. Dick would make a note and bring it into a meeting on Monday morning and we all would discuss the ideas for an hour. I learned real fast that not all PhDs are subject-matter experts on every subject. Dick and I had the job of testing some ideas that required building novel and one-of-a-kind engineering test fixtures.

I continued to work on watches at night. The work on watches wasn't for the money but to make friends who would do work for me, because if I had to go through the purchasing department to obtain a job requisition, it would take me maybe a week of paperwork to get an hour's work from a machine shop. When someone came to talk to me about watch repair, I didn't think I should spend too much time at GE's expense. I said to Dick if you think I'm spending too much time just tell me. He said, "If you stop working on watches, we'll be out of business." Dick gave me so many things to think about. I'd learn a lot about how a watch shop should work from school, but something Dick said always was the best policy. He said someone gives you a watch to repair. He complains it cost too much and it takes longer than it should have. But a year later when their watch needs repair again, the only thing the owner remembers was the good work you did. I could have made a livelihood, a good one just repairing watches, but I have a problem talking too much about the work to be done. I found my niche wasn't watches but making tools to make watch parts. I dearly loved the work.

I think as I write this no one has been as happy as I have at work. You might say I've never worked and I've played at what I wanted to do. What better job than at GE who let me play.

Dick kept busy with all the problems that needed to be solved from the Monday morning meetings. I'm a tinkerer, who likes to play at a job. Dick was an engineer who didn't work at a trade like I did. He did his work on paper. To Dick every job had to be worked out by a formula, which I didn't understand. Dick gave up on me trying to get me understand engineering, and I had enough in engineering school to know I'd never be an engineer like Dick. We had an unreal relationship. He would work the problem on paper and then tell me what he wanted me to do. It was a great feeling to know I was working with a great engineer. I'd been told that Dick was GE Space Department's best engineer. While everything was going great, Dick kept telling me GE in Cincinnati, Ohio, wants me transferred to the Jet Engine Department to make strain gages. The old watch makers are retiring, and I'm needed to see if I can get the machine working, which I invented back in 1955.

In a way, I was glad that Dick thought I would help him when he needed it most. I always knew he was different; everyone knew him from his eyeglasses. He had three pairs. He would shuffle those glasses, try a pair, take them off, and then try another pair. He was hard to work with. He had the reputation of being a smart engineer. He had two PhD's. He was about ten or twelve years older than me. Dick and I had a lot of conversations about life while just the two of us worked together for months. He told me he was a lawyer and a pharmacist.

Dick Ravenhall and I got to be the best of friends. In fact, after a few years we worked together, just the two of us were solving whatever problem that needed looked at. Dick was an "engineer's engineer," and he didn't work on problems at a work bench. He did his work with mathematics on a blackboard. Then he would tell what to do, and we worked as a team.

My Invention: Semiautomated Strain-Gage Production

——— ⌀ ———

AFTER THINKING ABOUT my love of strain gages, I'll have a lot to say about strain gages and my future lifetime after I've left GE.

I had to decide about what I was going to do. I questioned my work for GE and what I should be doing with my life. Hutchie didn't want to go back to Cincinnati, Ohio. Not that we didn't like Cincinnati, but the fact was that we were happy in West Chester, Pennsylvania. Dick wanted me to go back to school and attend a class that I'd heard about and I thought I'd enjoy it. The name of the class was "An Objective Way to Look at the Problem." In the first lecture, the teacher started out asking the question, "How does a washing machine work"? Everyone knows that the washing machine agitator goes back and forth. The agitator can also go up and down and wash clothes. The teacher asked, "How else can it work"? No one said anything. The teacher said, "How about if we hold the actuator and rotate the washing machine?" When he said that, I didn't hear anything he said after that.

The semiautomatic strain-gage winding machine was my big breakthrough.

I've been thinking about a different way to make a semiautomated strain-gage winder since I had the strain-gage winder made back in 1955. This class was just for me. After class that night, I went home and made a semiautomated strain-gage winder prototype out of simple materials. I used a 2"× 4" piece of wood and cut it into two pieces about 6" long. I made one piece for the base and the second piece with a hole through the center so I could turn the top piece. On the top piece, I drove five nails at one end and seven nails at the other end to thread. I pretended the thread was my strain-gage wire. The nails were the pins the wire was wrapped around. I was excited. I took this model to show Dick the next morning. I think he was as excited as I was.

The first thing Dick suggested was, "Don't the show semiautomated strain-gage winder prototype to anyone, and don't try to get a patent because nine times out of ten you would lose if GE wanted to take it to court."

Dick was so excited. He said, "Let me see what I can do for you." Now this was the time I've got to decide on not to transfer to the GE Jet Engine Department. Dick figured a way for me to receive twenty years' severance pay along with other benefits. He got all the benefits, insurance, investing plan, everything except the severance pay, and the company will pay my moving expense whenever I want to move and set up making gages for the Jet Engine Department.

I'm not good at making business decisions. Dick Ravenhall felt I had a good future developing my wonderful idea and thought I would make a good living making strain gages by running my own business. A part of my separation agreement was that I was obligated to make gages for the GE Jet Engine Department in Cincinnati, Ohio. Now after all that Dick had done for me, Hutchie didn't want to move back to West Virginia. In my mind, I was not as sure about the strain-gage future as Dick was.

If I decide to stay where I live in West Chester, Pennsylvania, to make strain gages, what will I do if my business fails?

Decision time.

I want to retire in Crab Orchard in the mountains of West Virginia.

My plan was to build a home in Crab Orchard, West Virginia. The spot I wanted was just across the valley from Hutchie's childhood home. It was a mountain peak where I wanted to spend the rest of my life.

The property owner would not commit to selling the land to me someday. This went on every year where we come to Crab Orchard, West Virginia, on vacation. I'd go see the property owner who owned thirty-six acres. I only wanted one acre on top of the mountain. My plan was to build a log cabin for my vacations and build a home when I retired from GE. I didn't expect to retire that soon. After six or seven years of visits, the property owner finally decided to sell an acre—just the acre I wanted.

After a few more vacations, I'd been clearing the one acre each vacation and I'd go see the owner of the adjacent lot who sold me the other thirty-five acres. Now I've got thirty-six acres of land and an old house on top of a mountain in West Virginia.

Now, I've got angels for a family—two wonderful girls, Dawn Louise aged thirteen and Lila Jane aged fifteen, and moved them into a cramped mobile home during a rainstorm when everything was muddy. The bedrooms were so small that you could hardly turn around in them.

Hutchie continued to let me know what she thought. I was at a low point in my life. I can't change things; I've already started the gage business, yet I was not happy. I was at a point where all my problems can't be true. I prayed, "Please Lord, make this a bad dream." I was tired after driving nine hours to West Chester, Pennsylvania, to pack up the family. Then things got much worse. While driving back to West Virginia, we experienced one of the worst rainstorms West Virginia ever had. The river was up in the road, and I had to detour around and the moving van went another way and got lost. I brought my family to the trailer, and these actions didn't help me at all. Now later in the day while raining cats and dogs, the van showed up. It got within two hundred feet of the old house where I was going to store our furniture and got stuck in the mud. We had to carry everything in the rain two hundred feet to the old house. Hutchie asked me why I decided to move there. I told her Dick Ravenhall told me that it would be a good business decision.

We finally settled into the old house to set up a strain-gage shop and the trailer to live in. This was the humble start of my new business: Strain-O-Therm Technology, Inc. Maybe I haven't made all the money I could have, but I've been doing something I love. I can now look at the good life I can give my family. Hutchie is now in a nice home, much better than we had in West Chester, Pennsylvania. Our home is located on top of a 2,800-foot-high mountain looking down on the little town of Crab Orchard, West Virginia and living there was like being in an airplane looking down on the town.

Strain-O-Therm Technology, Inc.

———— ❦ ————

I KNEW THE semiautomated strain-gage winder was a revolutionary invention and had an important future. I founded Strain-O-Therm Technology, Inc., my own high-temperature wire-wound strain-gage business, and worked it for forty-two years after I left General Electric.

In fact, GE became one of my largest customers. Go figure…

I was only thirty-seven years old and I was producing the highest quality, high-temperature strain gage in the world at the time and I kept the technology to myself as my trade secret. I always thought of the semiautomated strain-gage winding machine like a watch movement. You can see and tell the time but how does it work? I was selling the gage, not the time.

In 2002, I got a call from Dr. Orval Ayers, a famous rocket engineer at Red Stone Arsenal in Alabama. He wanted to see where the high-temperature wire-wound strain gages being used for their missile testing were coming from and traveled to see me in Crab Orchard, West Virginia. Dr. Orval Ayers wanted to know where Strain-O-Therm Technology, Inc. lab was and was surprised to see my home laboratory. I would not allow Dr. Orval Ayers to see my strain-gage winding machine to learn how it worked.

In the back of my mind, I've thought about strain gages almost every day. My work since 1961 has been the new foil gage. The work GE has in Cincinnati, Ohio, at the Jet Engine Department was the high-temperature wire strain gage. Dick kept asking me if I'd like to go to Ohio. It would be a pay raise. Now, I was enjoying work and didn't want to change. One day Dick came to me and said GE is putting pressure on him to send me to the Jet Engine Department.

In February 1971 Dick Ravenhall and I reached an agreement for Strain-O-Therm Technology, Inc. to produce strain gages for the GE Jet Engine Department in Cincinnati and send the gages to the Jet Engine Department in Cincinnati, Ohio.

My job now was to use my semiautomated strain-gage winding machine to make strain gages for GE Jet Engine Department. I got my tools together and made a work bench. I went

to Charleston, West Virginia, to get the brass material I was going to need to make a semiautomated strain-gage winding machine.

I had no doubts that I couldn't build the semiautomated strain-gage winding machine. I build
things in my mind and I know where I'm going from there. I felt like a lost kid not knowing how
this business was going to work out. I know I can make the machine, but I still had no clue how
much work will there be in the future.

I started to work building a strain-gage machine. I was really surprised when I found I could
design the machine to make the two different-sized gages that GE Jet Engine Department required. One gage was a 1/8" gage and the other was 1/16". I completed the machine in forty
working hours. When the semiautomated strain-gage winding machine was completed, I called
GE Jet Engine Department asking for a spool of strain-gage wire. I made a 1/8" gage and took it
to GE. Bill Binnethum, the manager of the strain-gage lab, saw the sample gage. I was surprised
when Bill was very happy with the quality of the strain gage.

At the time I didn't know. But Bill was a longtime friend in the gage business at the ANPD
and had a lot to do with my being laid off from GE to get me in the gage business. Bill liked the
quality of the gage and said it was ten times better than the hand-built gages at GE. GE gave me
an order for five hundred high-temperature wire wound-strain gages. Now, I have the world's
first semiautomated strain-gage winding machine and a big order from GE!

With my semiautomated strain-gage winding machine, I can make five hundred gages per
day. At GE, in 1954, the strain-gage lab had 150 watch repair men winding strain gages, and they
could only wind two good gages per day per person. I can make perfect gages in ten to fifteen
seconds on a semiautomated strain-gage winding machine.

Now, I've got an order for gages, and the good news was that it's not going to keep me busy
for long. I'm not the one to sit around, so I started to think about other projects. I'm expecting
fourteen hours of strain-gage work a month, so I'm going to have time on my hands.

I'd worked a great deal with a new field of photoelasticity in the industrial use of photoelastic reflection. My work in this field was pioneering. Vishay Micro Measurements dis-
covered that I was available through a friend Nick Nickola, whom I had worked with in the
ANPD in Cincinnati, Ohio. Nick is now with the photoelastic group. Nick asked me to make
some models for him. This meant I'd have to buy a large drill press and a large band saw.
Now this helped fill my time, but I was not happy as I was at the Apollo program. Next, Nick
asked me to instrument and apply some foil strain gages on some metal beams that would be

sent to an engineering school for practice stress work. This work was for Vishay Research and Education.

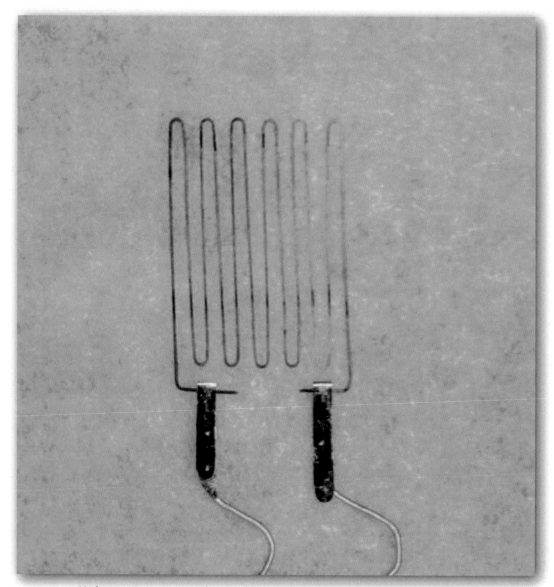

High-temp strain gage produced on a semiautomated strain-gage winding machine.
P. Allan Hill's wire-wound strain gage is incredibly small. This strain gage's wire diameter is
0.0008 inch, 0.26 the diameter or one-fourth the diameter of a human hair.
Allan made thousands of strain gages!
(Photo by Vince Wnuk, Hi Tech Products, Inc., the company
that acquired Strain-O-Therm Technology, Inc.)

It seems like everything in my life was temporary now. I was making money now, but life isn't right without my family. My dream for years has been some day to develop a semiautomated machine to make the high-temperature strain gages. That dream was in my mind ever since I got the patent on the strain gage back in 1955. Now maybe this new machine will be a big part in my future. I'm not sure about the business, but I only knew that I can make a semiautomated machine. After a couple weeks, GE hasn't ordered any more gages. I was concerned about the future for the strain-gage business.

I started getting more strain-gage orders from GE in Cincinnati and the work for Vishay Photo Elastic was only a part-time job. I was going to need more income to make my dream of the dream house come true. The type work from Vishay is only temporary, and I wanted more to make the income for the dream home. My thoughts were that I've got these thirty-six acres of land with a house trailer. I remember driving home from West Chester, Pennsylvania, to Crab Orchard, West Virginia, and I saw a small mobile home park, which looked nice. Maybe with the land I had, it could be developed into a mobile home park and provide extra income to the family. So, thinking someday the strain-gage business might fail, it would be nice to have an income. I took a trip down into the woods where I thought the mobile home development could be built. I didn't know anything about my property; I hadn't looked it over since I'd bought it. I would see if could I cut some trees and do some landscaping and it'll be a perfect place for a mobile home park. So now I'll have to see about the zoning for a mobile home park and familiarized myself with the laws and regulations. Hutchie sold our home in West Chester, Pennsylvania, while I was at Crab Orchard, West Virginia, building my first semiautomated strain-gage winding machine. We paid $16,500 in 1961. We sold it in 1971 and made a nice profit. Hutchie was very good at managing money. That's the reason I've got some now.

Not everyone thinks the way I do, not Hutchie, not her family. Papaw Horton, Hatchie's father, took me to see a lawyer to get all the details for building a mobile home park. The lawyer said to Papaw while I was sitting there, "Talk him out of the trailer park. It's not a good idea. I'm already representing eight people who started and failed." The family thought I was crazy, but the more people complained about my building a mobile home park, I had my mind made up. Dad and I didn't get along about much; he did teach me how to go about getting what you want. That wonderful home I want for my family won't come easy. It'll take time and more money than I have now. With my plans, this park will make the extra money I'll need to build the dream home on top of the hill. The park income will be around $2,000 per month, and when I get the gage business going, I'll be on my way to build my dream home.

Waterlines and sewer lines must be dug out. I did it myself. This I learned from the hard work Dad had taught me as a young boy. This was the year 1971, and I was forty-three years old and as strong and healthy as any young man, so I put myself to work as hard as I could take.

The mobile park was coming along fine except when I had 50 percent completed, my year was up with the contract I'd made with GE. After I'd been gone from GE for one year, I had to go back and work a month to get all my benefits. While back at GE in Philadelphia Apollo Project, my old manager wanted me to come back to work. I asked him how could he ask me since Dick Ravenhall got the severance deal for me a year earlier. But he said, "I'm still your manager and I want you back." Now what do I do?

The park was only 50 percent complete. My family wasn't one bit happy living in the small trailer. I've already found it's going to be hard for me to get money for the home I've dreamed of all these years. The strain-gage business hasn't yet been what I was going to need to support my family the way we lived in Philadelphia, Pennsylvania.

So, what do I do now?

Jet Engine Fan Blade Testing and High-Temperature Strain Gages

It turned out that the research and development of jet engine turbine fan blades require lots of high-temperature wire wound strain gages, and I had the world's first semiautomated strain-gage winding machine.

Business for Strain-O-Therm Technology, Inc. is now looking better!

I decided to go home and someday build that dream home I'd planned. I completed the mobile home park. Hutchie helped me with marketing materials, and I made a sample strain gage and sent it out to all the Society for Experimental Mechanics (SEM) members I knew who would be using the wire strain gage. A few days later I got a call from Pratt & Whitney Jet Engine Division in West Palm Beach, Florida, research department. Pratt & Whitney was a company I knew nothing about, but it didn't take me long to learn. I jumped on my motorcycle and took off to Pratt & Whitney Jet Engine Division in Florida. The work orders for my strain gages was far greater than the GE Jet Engine Department. Then one of those odd things that just happens.

My semiautomated strain-gage winding machine I'd just fabricated for GE's 1/8" gage, the only size I ever thought would be used for, was adjustable and I found that I could also make 1/8" and 1/16" gage on the same machine. Up until now I was going to get my biggest order from GE's Lynn, Massachusetts, smaller jet engines for 1/16" gages. GE in Cincinnati large Jet Engine Department wanted to know if I could heat treat thin gages. The temperature had to be 1,040 degrees Fahrenheit for two hours. I had to buy a furnace for heat-treating. Heat treating a strain gage took more time, and I charged more for each gage. My time to make a gage was about two minutes longer to heat treat.

I worked almost full time, applying foil gages for General Motor's Allison Engine Company in Indianapolis, Indiana. The lab manager, Dock Cunningham, was trying to help me sell my wire gage, with no luck, but they had a union and made their own wire gages. One day I got a call from the general manager of the General Motor's Allison Engine Company telling me they wanted to have a meeting next day at 9:00 a.m. I jumped on my motorcycle and rode down to Louisville, Kentucky, and then up to Allison the next day to see Dock Cunningham. We sat down at a big table with eight to ten engineers. Dock felt it's important to find a way to supply the General Motor's Allison Engine Company's Jet Engine Department with wire strain gages, and they needed to know how I made the strain gages.

We talked and talked, and got nowhere. My only answer was, "I'll supply you with all the strain gages you'll need, and I'm the only one in the world with semiautomated strain-gage winding machine." I added my machine was like a watch. "You can look at it and tell the time. Similarly, you can look at my machine, but there is no way you can see the workings inside." Dock was almost telling me it was my duty to let him know how my machine worked. I was getting the feeling they thought I was a dumb West Virginia boy, and they can talk me into telling them what they wanted to know. After listening patiently to some of the smart questions, I was getting mad, and I was not too bright when I get mad, so I picked up my briefcase and told them, "It's a very simple process. I use horse manure and rubber bands." I got the order!

A few weeks after that meeting, the General Motor's Allison Engine Company was acquired by the Rolls-Royce Company. I got an order from Rolls-Royce for heat-treated wire gages, just like GE. Rolls-Royce wanted the gages heat treated, as GE wanted, at 1,040 degrees Fahrenheit, but Rolls-Royce also wanted their gages heated for three hours. Before I could get the order, I had to bring my oven to their lab and have them certify it. It was about the size of a kitchen oven, so I loaded it up and took it to their loading dock.

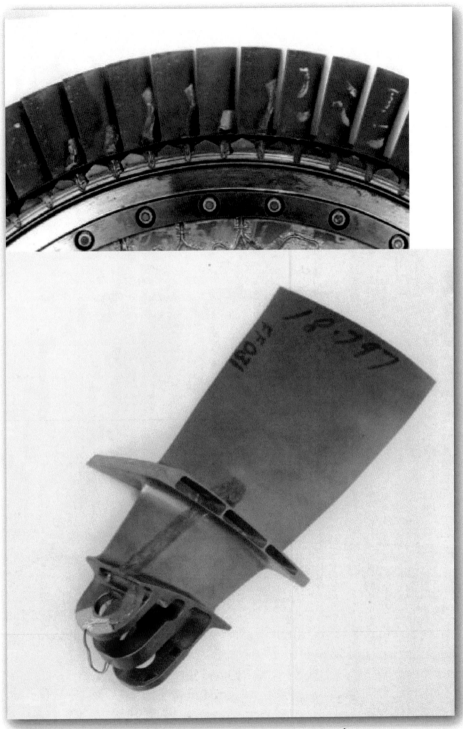

A jet turbine fan with wire strain gages mounted.

I got the Rolls-Royce order. I was now supplying every jet engine manufacturer who uses wire strain gages with my semiautomated strain-gage winding machine. I didn't think business could be any better than this.

P. Allan Hill's high-temperature strain gages were used in the development and testing of this massive GE jet engine.

At one of my Society of Experimental Mechanics meetings, I met Mr. Steve Wnuk from Hi-Tech Corporation in Boston, Massachusetts. Hi-Tech was a company that did contract work for GE–Pratt & Whitney Jet Engine Division or anyone who wanted high-temperature strain-gage work. When GE or Pratt & Whitney Jet Engine Division had more work than they could handle, Hi-Tech got the work, so I got to know everyone at Hi-Tech. At one meeting Steve Wnuk, one of the four owners took me to lunch and explained some changes in their operation. Steve sold his stake in the company and formed his own subsidiary of Hi-Tech Corporation, which will continue to do contract work, and Steve's new company will be Hi-Tech Products, Inc. While talking, Steve said, "You would be selling me all the strain-gage Hi-Tech uses." He added, "I've got an order for one hundred each 1/8" un-flattened gages." This was on a Saturday, and Steve told me, "I'll need them by the end of next week." I replied, "Steve, I'll be home Monday and you'll have the gages by 10:30 a.m. Tuesday." He said, "You don't understand. It's one hundred gages." My answer surprised him. "If I get an order I can make approximately five hundred a day, and if I mail them out before 5:00 p.m., you'll get the gages by 10:30 p.m. the next day."

With this new company, Steve will supply material used in high-temperature work to all companies that use wire, high-temperature gages. Some call them gages for hostile environment. Now, I'm getting more and more contract work, but my wire strain gages always come first. Although I don't even remember any problems with any other job, I had things going my way. When a company would call, and ask for a quote, I'd give them one and tell them the delivery would be within ten days of the purchase order. This way when they called for a quote, I knew they wanted the gage. I started making gages for that order as soon as they called. So if I got busy doing something else, I'd have the order ready.

It's a great knowing I was the only source of quality high-temperature strain gages. I got an order from France asking for a quote for one hundred gages. They wouldn't provide anything in English, only French. I said if you can't give me a part number or product nomenclature in English, I won't give you any gages. They responded with a no and I was firm too. About a month later, Steve Wnuk, Hi-Tech Products, called and asked why I won't supply France with gages. I said, "I'll sell you gages and you can supply them, but I'm not going to give you the discount." We did the deal.

That was the real beginning of Strain-O-Therm Technology, Inc. We met at the next SEM meeting and discussed the strain-gage material. Steve said Hi-Tech Products knows the world market and asked me, "Why don't you let us be your agent for the strain-gage market?" We talked and talked. Then we argued Hi-Tech Products would take Pratt & Whitney Jet Engine Division and the world market. I'd keep General Electric, Rolls-Royce Company, and NASA. I didn't know if there were more companies overseas that needed my strain gage than there were in the United States. My strain-gage business was beyond Dick Ravenhall's dreams. If only Dick was around to help me with business.

The last thirty years I've worked producing high-temperature strain gages about one and half days a week. Other than that, I've been very busy with foil strain-gage work, which has more than filled up my week, and some jobs have kept me working all weekend long. When I make a wire gage, sometimes I look at the machine and wonder why someone else can't know how to do something that will make a gage. I think if the market was bigger, someone would try to make a machine.

I'm just lucky that I'm the one who is now doing it. I'm now eighty-eight years old and I'm afraid the market will disappear as soon as all new ideas are developed. I'm a tinkerer. I don't know anything about the new electric gadgets, but I do think maybe the life of wire-type strain gage might be over soon.

NASA Supersonic Transport Project

NASA WAS GOING to build a top-secret new plane. The Supersonic Transport (SST) was the first step before the NASA's space shuttle to take astronauts into space. This was a very important project at the time.

The testing on the SST was done on tile stress and temperature. The strain gages I made did both, and Langley was satisfied with the performance of the gages. But the project came to an end, due to a government budget decision. I think someday it'll be brought back to be fabricated for space travel. Beginning in the early 1960s, NASA commenced the SCAT (Supersonic Commercial Air Transport) program, which based most of its research from the North American XB-70 Valkyrie program.

Some of my best ideas come from the Society of Experimental Mechanics meetings I went to. There was a meeting somewhere once a year, and I tried to attend it. One meeting I went to was one close to West Virginia. It was at Oak Ridge, Tennessee. The topic of the meeting was the "China" alloy. I was very interested in this meeting. The "China" wire is a big interest in strain-gage wire. Each company is trying to find a better wire for gages. Each company supplied me with the wire they want me to use for the gages. I've been getting orders for gages of the China wire with instruction to be careful because the wire is expensive. It cost forty dollars per inch. Some of the companies had ordered thousands of dollars' worth of wire and had to pay first to get the wire. China stopped letting the United States have it. There were four engineers who were delivering papers on the "China" wire. As always, I end up with Bill Binnumthon, a GE engineer, who was one of the outstanding authoritative persons in the field of hostile or high-temperature strain gages. I was seated beside Bill when he asked me if I'm giving one of the "China" alloy papers. I said, "I'm the only gage supplier, and I made all the Chinese gages." Everyone knows Bill. So the engineer in the seat in front of me turned to Bill and said, "Who the hell is he?" I never know how to take that, but no one knows Allan Hill. Bill turned to me and told the engineer, "This is Allan Hill with Strain-O-Therm Technology." At that point, the man sitting in front of Bill said to me, "We have got to get together before we leave the meeting." No one knows Allan Hill but everyone knows Strain-O-Therm, Inc. That made me feel good.

The man who asked Bill, "Who the hell is this man?" was none other than Dr. Bill Sharpe. He was the head of engineering at Johns Hopkins University. The engineer beside Sharpe was Dr. Hossele, head of engineering at Pratt & Whitney Jet Engine Division. Dr. Hossele took me to lunch and told me there was going to be some new NASA work, which is going to need wire such as the China alloy. He has an ingot of material, which he thought, is the same as the China alloy. He said, "When the ingot is made into wire at the Cole Fine Wire Company we want you to make some gages for us." This wire was made just for one job. The wire was called BCH-3 wire.

This was the beginning of a big project. Langley just about lived at my lab while I made all different gages that they required. Some were good tests, but some were not so good. Dr. Mike Lemcoe was the engineer from Edwards NASA base. Dr. Lemcoe would come in and say this is the type gage they needed to get the test results they need. I can't say that it didn't work because it's already tried by Langley NASA. Some days later Dr. Lemcoe came in and was not happy with the way the testing was proceeding. He said to me, "I'm going to get the government to sue you because it has millions of dollars in this project." I could care less about NASA, but GE put me in this business, and it's like family to me. If someone gets the business, I want to know whether they will always keep the gage business as great as I have.

The Sale of Strain-O-Therm Technology, Inc.

My hard work pays off!

I GOT TO thinking about the future and wanted to slow down and enjoy life. Hi-Tech Products, Inc. had expressed the desire to buy my strain-gage business.

Selling a pig in a poke isn't an easy job. I can't reveal the inner workings of my semiautomatic strain-gage machine.

This took a few weeks because the bank didn't want to let Hi-Tech Products have the money just because they wanted the money. We reached a deal. I was not entirely happy because I loved the work but at seventy-four years, I can't work forever. This is the company that should have the business.

The best part was when Steve Wnuk asked me if I would continue making the gages for them. That was music to my ears. I did that for another ten years. I called Steve to come and pick up everything. I kept some things I'd need, which were not strain gage related. I had eighteen microscopes, and I kept five for some projects I wanted to work on. When I sold Steve the company, he gave me an order for five hundred gages. I went up to Boston for a meeting with Hi-Tech the next week. I took the five hundred gages. I told Steve, "I've never asked who your customers were, because I didn't think I should know who they were." Steve said one hundred gages are going to the GE Schenectady, New York, research center, two hundred are going to Greensboro, South Carolina, where GE is building a turbine for a cruise ship. The other two hundred are going to China.

Now I'm working at what I enjoy and have no worries about the future. My money is in the bank, and I'm still making strain gages. Steve is a better businessman than me. He raised the price of gages almost twice of what I charged.

What more can you expect than being happy with your work and having a loving family?

I've got it all.

I have a blessing not many people can have.

Motorcycle Trips: My Love for a Motorcycle Goes a Long Way Back

P. Allan Hill and his younger brother, David Hill, in West Virginia enjoying
a ride on April 9, 1947, while Allan was home on leave from the US Navy.

MY FIRST BIKE was 1928 Harley Davidson. I don't remember much about the bike, and I didn't have it for long. I was fifteen years old. Dad had me working and he paid me a good wage. This was 1943 or 1944 and I bought the bike for fifty dollars. When Dad took a job to do, he wouldn't take it unless I would be his helper. Dad demanded top dollar for me. I always had money. I bought the bike near Saulsville, West Virginia. The name of the town was Tipple, which is no longer there. I rode the bike approximately five miles and it stopped. There was a friend with me so we pushed it to the top of the hill and I drifted down the other side to Mabin, West Virginia. I couldn't get it started again. I had someone with a pick-up truck get it and take it to Princeton, West Virginia, Harley Davidson motorcycle shop.

Later that year I found another bike I'd like to have. It was a very unusual bike. It was a 1939 Harley Davidson with four hundred miles, like new. It was a big bike, in fact, the largest bike made. It had been a police bike. It had a single seat and lots of lights, with the word "Police" written on the tanks. I never knew why the police had a big bike; they should have had a small one. The bike was the most powerful bike around. It was a 1,300 cc engine and I wanted it. I remember the bike cost me $400, but that would be like $4,000 today. I wanted the bike bad but didn't have the money. Dad said I've got a job for you. School was out and he wanted me to work through summer. He had a job and he was building a basement for the local church. He asked, "How bad do you want the motorcycle?" I was ready to work if Dad would buy the bike. The next morning $400 was on the breakfast table. I went to Beckley, West Virginia, to pick up the bike, and at that time no one needed license to ride motorcycles.

School started and I rode the bike to school on days when the weather would permit. I did enjoy the bike. I got to know friends who liked to ride and on the weekends, we saw a lot of West Virginia. My education was somewhat different than most boys my age. While at Basin, West Virginia, I went to Herndon High School for six months. Then we moved to Stephenson (Devils Fork), West Virginia, and I went to the school at Mullens, West Virginia. Some way I ended up in the ninth grade the second time.

I was now seventeen years old. It was Thanksgiving time. I was in the ninth grade and had nothing but Fs. I had only one C, and it was in Health. The principal called me into his office and said, "You can't finish school at the rate you're going." He asked, "What do you intend to do with your life?" My answer was, "I want to ride a motorcycle to South America," and he said, "I think you should start now!"

In December 1945, I rode my motorcycle to Bluefield, West Virginia, to join the navy. The temperature was in the low forties and it got colder the farther I went. My fingers got so cold and I had a hard time taking my gloves off so I could get gas. The navy said I'd have to have Dad sign some papers. So, Dad took me back to Bluefield, West Virginia. A few days later, in January, I joined the navy.

I rode my motorcycle to Camp Perry, Virginia, and after boot camp I rode home. While on the ride in Rhodell, West Virginia, I stopped to talk to someone. A man walked by and told me how he lost a leg on a motorcycle accident, but he could still ride. He jumped on my bike and went down the road out of sight. Soon thereafter a man asked me if the motorcycle belonged to me. I walked down the road to where the motorcycle was. A pick-up truck had run into the back of the bike. The rear wheel was pushed under the seat. The rider had started to turn around and killed the engine. He was off the road where it stopped. The pick-up truck hitting the back of the bike caused lots of damage. It was a complete loss. The truck driver was drunk. He pleaded me not to call the police. This driver was a man who worked at the blacksmith shop at the mine with Dad. He said, "I'll take care of everything for you." The motorcycle was taken to the Princeton, West Virginia, Harley shop for repairs.

I was now back in the US Navy. Dad called to tell me the bike had been repaired and he sold it for more than I'd paid for it. I was discharged from the navy early because the war was over. The first thing I needed was transportation. I was discharged on December 17. When I got home, it wasn't motorcycle weather. I bought a car, but not for long. I had signed up to go to the school of horology in Pittsburgh, Pennsylvania, which started six months later. On August 1, after a few warm days, I was thinking it was motorcycle weather. I traded the car for a 1947 740HV Harley Davidson. A new bike with all the trimmings. It was beautiful. I could see I couldn't have a car at school, and with the motorcycle I could ride home from Pittsburgh, Pennsylvania, each week after school if the weather was good. For a few trips, the weather wasn't that good, but I was happy that I got to ride.

Riding was not my only thought. I had a cute little sweetheart named Lila Lee Horton (a.k.a Hutchie) who liked to ride with me. The school lasted until June 1950, and I had some trips I'll never forget.

It's about three hundred miles from Crab Orchard, West Virginia, to Pittsburgh, Pennsylvania, and sometimes I'd get home early enough to go for a ride over to the drug store and get a coke. I tried to start back Sunday around one or two in the afternoon. One afternoon the rain was coming down. I started north in the direction of Prince Railroad station. The weather was beginning to look bad so I thought I would go to Charleston, West Virginia, and take Route 2 up the river.

I got over to about Oak Hill, West Virginia, and now the weather was looking worse than up Rt. 19. So, I went back to Prince station and up Rt. 19. I don't remember what town it was, but it started to hail like I'd never seen before. I had an army blanket on my motorcycle seat. I put the blanket over my head to protect it from the golf ball sized hail. Of course, I stopped the bike. When I got to the town, the tree branches had been torn down into the street and all water drains on the street had been stopped up and the water in the street was eight or ten feet deep. This wasn't a good day for a ride. That was one ride that I'll never forget.

Another ride I remember was coming home one night from Pittsburgh, Pennsylvania. It was later than usual. I was on Rt. 2 along the Ohio River. The full moon was out and the temperature was about 71 degrees Fahrenheit and I was enjoying the night so much that I wanted to just keep riding. It was a night I've thought of many times. I've tried to relive it. That was the year 1948 or 1949. I had motor problems with the bike and I couldn't afford the repair cost and sold the bike to Buddie Jones, a wonderful motorcycle friend. After school, I joined the Army Air Force, which changed to US Air Force during the first week I was in it. I was sent to England after thirty days in the Air Force.

While in England I'd tell the boys how I enjoyed riding. There were two boys who also liked to ride. They bought bikes alike. The bike was Vincent HRD Bikes. These are probably the best in the world at the time. One of the boys took a two-hundred-mile bike trip to London and had an accident and broke his leg. His friend with the other HRD bike asked me if I would ride with him to London to see our friend in the hospital. I said yes. I never knew how anyone riding on the back of a motorcycle felt. Boy, I'm glad this boy was a good motorcycle driver. The roads in England are narrow and had lots of curves. What a ride. That was the last time I was on a bike until 1974 or 1975.

A man in our mobile home park wanted to sell me his bike. I wanted a bike, but now life was different. I've got a family, which comes first. I really hadn't thought about a bike for years because I was busy working and I had two girls to send to college. I told the man with the bike to ask my brother, David, if he wants the bike, so that's where he went. David said to the man, "Take the bike to Allan and tell him it's his birthday present." This isn't the way life is meant to be. I called David and ask why and he said, "You know three or four years ago, I built a radio tower on your hill and I owe you $470 per month for three years for the tower." The bike was like new and in fact was driven less than five hundred miles. The bike was a small bike; it was a 500 cc Honda, one of the odd things about the bike was it was the first Honda with a water-cooled engine and a drive shaft, not a chain.

I was back at motorcycle riding. I found three more friends who had bikes like mine. These were not the high-powered motorcycles like the Hell's Angels ride. But we sure did enjoy them. Our first trip on the Honda 500 was over to Houston up to Oklahoma City and back home. On our first day, we went up to Montgomery, Alabama, and the two thin men of our group stayed in Houston.

With two of the men, I went to Waco, Texas, to spend the night with a good friend from the Air Force. Not everyone could go on like we did, but my friend Obe and I had talked about this type of thing and it was what he wanted. Obe was my right hand when it came to my work in the Air Force. Obe's wife Betty and my wife Hutchie were close friends, and Obe and I spent many hours on the weekends fishing.

Now Obe is a rancher with a sixteen-thousand-acre ranch. We went fishing in one of Obe's lakes. The men on this trip were two brothers Denis and Euile Riffe, Arnold Deck, John Morgan, and me. The two brothers said they would meet Arnold, John, and me at a Holiday Inn on Rt. 35, so the three of us got to the hotel early. We waited for hours. We didn't have cell phones back then. I called home to tell Hutchie where we are and asked whether the two brothers called. They did and we met up again and went up to Henrietta, Oklahoma, to spend the night, and over to Memphis, Tennessee, to spend the next night with my good friend, Don Horton, who was Hutchie's brother. This was the middle of April and the weather was great. But that morning in Memphis, the temperature was forty-six degrees, and it got colder as we got closer to home. That part of the trip was 640 miles from Memphis to Crab Orchard. I had a large beach towel that I wrapped around me under my coat, but my fingers froze. It was 42 degrees when we got to Crab Orchard, West Virginia.

Our next trip was to Daytona Beach, Florida. Daytona is where all the motorcyclists meet before the Daytona 500 stock car race. On another trip with four guys, we went down to Key West, Florida. On the way home, we got to Jacksonville, Florida. The moon was bright and the temperature was just right. Gene Deck said, "Wouldn't it be great to ride all night?" I thought about the time I was riding down the Rt. 2 along the Ohio River, and I said, "Let's do it." We had our 500 cc bikes for a while now and I remember how hard we rode that night and they never failed. If we burn these bikes up, we will need a new one. I didn't really mean it, but we are ready for bigger bikes, which would carry more weight than smaller bikes.

One nice weekend I had a cookout for my motorcycle friends. When I got onto my bike for another ride, my short legs didn't go over the seat. I just knocked my bike over into Hutchie's flower bed. I found a 1975 Honda 1000 cc, which had so many extras that they cost as much as the bike. The bike had five hundred miles on it, and the price was low for that type of a bike.

The first trip on this bike was with my two friends, Gene Deck and Denis Riffe. We went up to the New Brunswick and Nova Scotia area in Canada. From there we rode southwest to New Hampshire. We were just riding and making no plans, when we needed fuel. We stopped at the foot of Mt. Washington, not knowing where we were. The employee at the gas station said, "You sure have a beautiful day to go up the mountain." We did and it was once-in-a-lifetime experience. The odd thing about the ride up the mountain was due to the weather we couldn't have gone the day before or the day after.

Our next trip was out West. Up until this time we hadn't been on any long trips. Our first sights to see was the Grand Canyon, which was a great sight to see. We were on a motorcycle ride to see everything we could see. This trip was with Gene Deck, Denis Riffe, Arnold Deck, and myself. Our next site to see was to ride the Death Valley. At the beginning of the Death Valley ride, we stopped to take pictures of the Death Valley sign. Denis parked his motorcycle away from the sign so he could get in the picture. But when Denis started to get on his bike, it was sunk into the sand. We lifted it out and continued to get gas, to make sure we had gas for the next day. At the gas station, it was about 4:00 p.m. and a car came in from the eastern part of California. The man said, "The winds are bad night now and I don't think you should go today." We got a room and stayed the night. We started early next day out. It was another wonderful ride, but we were so glad we didn't ride the Death Valley at night because we wouldn't have seen all the beautiful sights.

We wanted to ride in the Yosemite Park the next day, but the information we got was it had snowed and the roads are closed. We continued to ride in that direction. When we got there the roads were open, but you couldn't visit anywhere. Arnold Deck got off and laid in the snow, making designs in the snow, while we took pictures. Another great day on a bike. Next day we went to Sacramento, California, and over to the Pacific Ocean. Gene Deck was excited about seeing the Pacific Ocean for the first time. He took his shoes off and waded out into the water while we took pictures. Something happened at the beach that day we still talk about when we get together. Rt. 1 goes north and south on Rt. 1 goes up the coast. We are inland in California and when we got to Rt. 1 we wanted to go north. When we get to Rt. 1 and got to the right, we were down the road a mile or so and Arnold said, "Men, we are going South." No way was our answer. But about that time a road sign said "South," so we turned around and went the other way, but we wanted to go back and see how that could be. From the ocean, we took Rt. 101 north to Red Wood National Park. We spent a day there and took a photo of us riding our bikes through a large tree. The size of these trees surprised me. From there we went to White Sands National Park in New Mexico. I think our next stop would be on the way home.

We took many short trips on our motorcycles, sometimes two or three of us, and one with thirty-seven riders. One weekend, thirty-seven riders wanted to ride the wonderful parkway in Virginia and Tennessee. We got on the Parkway at Rt. 60 in Virginia. We rode north to the New Market exit. On the park way, approximately five miles north of the New Market exit, thirty-two of the riders went around a curve, five of us come to the curve. Then a deer jumped into Marvin Lively's lap while he was driving on the motorcycle. Marvin wrecked, and he lay on top the deer, which was dead by now. One biker behind Marvin went around Marvin and the deer. I was next. I had to lay my bike down to keep from running over Marvin, and a bike behind me had to lay his down to keep from running over me. Another thing that happened, which you can't explain, was Marvin lying in the ditch. He was hurt and we didn't want to make him worse, but as we were thinking about what to do, a doctor came by with a telephone to call for help. He had a large blanket in his suburban van. He made Marvin as comfortable as possible. Howard Riffe and I stayed with Marvin until he was taken to the hospital. The other men went looking for the other thirty-two riders. They had stopped to eat, thinking we would be along soon. We didn't have cell phones back in those days to call the other riders in the group.

We took weekend trips to Hungry Mother State Park in Kentucky. As I'm writing this, I must wonder when any of us had time to work. As for me, my strain-gage business kept me busy one and a half days a week. Hutchie managed the trailer park business. For my strain-gage business when I got a quote, I knew they wanted a gage. I'd answer by saying I'll have the gage ready within ten days after I receive a purchase order from the customer. What a life. One day Arnold Deck called me and wanted to go for a ride. I hadn't been to some of the northern states, so we started up Rt. 75 to Sault Sainte Marie, Michigan and then took Rt. 2 across the United States to Spokane, Washington. I told Arnold, "I've been in all the states now except Alaska, so let's go back home."

I rode my motorcycle in all the contiguous US states.

This was something I really wanted to say. I had been to all the states on a motorcycle. Would you believe the pastor of our church said, "Let's take a good long ride and I'll show you men places you have never seen?" Phil Shields, our pastor, had been a truck driver as a young man and had been all over the United States. Our pastor asked Gene Deck, Denis Riffe, Howard Riffe, Phil Shields, and me to go. Phil was going to lead us to wherever he wanted to go. First, we went to Sault St. Marie, Michigan. From there, we took the same Rt. 2, which I'd been on the year before. At Coeur d'Alene, Idaho, there was road repair. They didn't do repair work like anyone else. They tore up the whole road and you must ride through the mud. On a motorcycle, you might have the front wheel in a deep wheel track a truck has made and your back wheel is in another track and this was not fun. Denis Riffe dropped his bike going two or three miles per hour. Denis got dirty and so did his bike. There wasn't anyone clean after we left Idaho. We rode over to the coast in Washington and then down from Seattle, we took Route 101 over to the coast. From the coast, we took Rt. 101 all the way down to California. Phil's brother was an Oregon state senator who took us up to the top of the Capital building, and you could see everything.

It was a wonderful experience. We went to Mt. St. Helens. You must see it to believe what a volcanic eruption can do.

Phil wanted us to see some of the beauty of this world. Just a few weeks before this trip, Gene called me and said, "I got a new motorcycle and let us go for a ride." I said, "OK, I can go for six days." So, we took off and rode to El Paso, Texas. Then we turned around and started home. We got to Shreveport, Louisiana, to spend the night. Gene said, "I've been here working, and if we get to up early in the morning, we can be home Saturday night and can go to church Sunday." We got up early to get started, and we got to Crab Orchard, West Virginia, around 10:00 p.m. We rode our motorcycles 978 miles that day!

Some people just think of, but never do. "Let's go to Alaska."

Here is another Phil Shields motorcycle adventure trip. Phil got Gene Deck, Denis Riffe, and me to plan "a trip of all motorcycle trips." First, we had to apply for our US passport, so that we could enter Canada. We had a meeting with some motorcycle friends who had made the trip.

There were so many problems which we didn't think of, and it was good we discussed things before the trip. Road conditions can be tricky at different times of the year. Motel rooms had to be made each day so we would have a room the next day. Gas stops had to be planned, because you don't know when the next gas station might be. You need tents just in case you can't get a motel. I got a scout ax and some material to start a fire. I didn't know what to expect, and was prepared. I had a large motorcycle trailer and it was going to be loaded when we would decide all the things we want to take. We will need tools for repairs if necessary. I'll have a couple tires. We will need oil for three of us. Denis has a new Harley and it will be serviced at the Harley dealer when we get there. The three of us will need to change oil at five thousand miles. All our bikes use the same oil. The tires are another problem. I've got an extra five-gallon gas tank on my motorcycle when it was converted to a trike. But I have a can of gas in the trailer just in case. With all our planning complete, on June 1, we got started.

All of us are from the Crab Orchard Baptist Church, and Phil Shields is our pastor. Phil will be our guide and he's a great leader. I'm the oldest member of the four. I was seventy-nine years on this ride. The first day out from West Virginia, we rode all the way to Nebraska. The next day we rode to Cheyenne, Wyoming, where we encountered our first problem. There was a large horse show in Cheyenne and all motel rooms were booked. We couldn't find a place where we could pitch our tents close to town. We decided to leave in a northern direction, looking for a place to pitch our tents. We found one about fifty or sixty miles north of Cheyenne. One problem there was it had room only for two tents. Phil had some medical problems so he needed one.

Denis and Gene had one large tent so they need one spot. I was left out. Gene and Denis let me put my bag in their tent. I slept under the stars that night.

We wanted to visit Phil's friend in Montana, but we stayed in a motel where he lived and from there we were going to start on our Alaska trip. We took US Rt. 15 up to Canada where we used our US passports. From there we took the Alaska Highway all the way to Fairbanks, Alaska. We enjoyed all the places in between. The road had some bad places, but not so bad that we didn't enjoy the ride. We changed oil in Fairbanks, Alaska.

One thing I'll always remember is how wonderful the people were in Alaska. Denis took his bike to the Harley Davidson shop for service and asked the manager where he could get his cell phone repaired. She said, "Give it to me; I'll take care of it." The phone repair area was a mile or more where she took it, got it repaired, and brought it back. Gene, Phil, and I need to change our oil. The Harley manager said, "We can't do it for you, but there is an area beyond our lot where you can do it, but please keep the area clean." This would require something to put our used oil in. The manager had someone bring us a tub and they took care of it. What wonderful people.

We went to Anchorage to meet some of Gene's friends. They told us about how much fun it is to watch the whales, but to get there it would be a few miles. I thought it might be a good idea to leave my trailer at their house while we rode to see the whales. We took off to watch the whales. After a few miles, Phil said he was getting low on fuel. These new bikes have all the new communication devices, and we talked to each other all the time. Phil reported that his fuel red light is on. So, he stopped. Phil thought I had extra fuel in a can, but my can is in my trailer. You could have made a movie about all the work that took place to get Phil fuel. I had extra fuel in my big fuel tanks on my trike. But how do we get to it? Someone had a pop bottle. Gene had a small rubber hose so they started getting some fuel in the bottle, enough for the red light to go off. There was a gas station not far down the road so it wasn't a problem.

Our next problem was that the road ahead was closed because of a fire in the woods and we had to go back to Anchorage, Alaska, to get my trailer and then start back home.

We got to see the wonderful sight of Mount McKinley standing at 20,320 ft. It rained hard one day when we got to Chicken Town, Alaska, and unfortunately we got there at a bad time just as a tour bus pulled in. The bad part was the long wait to go to the one outdoor bathroom. All of us said we would like to go back to Chicken Town, Alaska, if there weren't so many people. Our next stop was at a roadside sign telling us we were at the "top of the world." I didn't think I'd ever get the boys to leave.

We were told the Mount McKinley park gate where we had to show our passport would close at 5:00 p.m. and it was getting close to five now. We could see the gate, but if it was closed we would have to go back in the rain maybe one hundred miles to get a room. So we took a long dry ride down the mountain to the Yukon and then to Dawson, Canada.

The Yukon was worth the trip just to see it. We had to take a boat across the Yukon. It was big and moving fast very fast. When the boat went to the other side, it didn't go straight across but down the river a long way because of the fast-moving water. There was a long line waiting to get across. We thought we would have to wait for hours, but someone came to us and told us to come to the front of the line. When the boat was loaded with cars and motor homes, they can always make room for motorcycles. We stayed at Dawson that night. From there we took the western road back.

I think on the ride from Canada into Idaho, I saw the most beautiful country I've ever seen. Phil wanted to go another way to see a friend, but we were ready to come home. Phil had to use a tire I had in the trailer. We changed it and from there we went home without Phil. He had a family reunion in Colorado.

My good friend, Gene Deck, has a saying about motorcycle riders: "You don't see a motorcycle parked outside a psychiatrist office"!

At age seventy-nine I rode a motorcycle 10,400 miles from West Virginia to Alaska and back in only eighteen days averaging 577 miles per day!

Going to Alaska on my motorcycle was a wonderful trip.

Dr. Lemcoe, who is funding Dr. Roger Adelman's work on a new speaker for a cell phone, called one day and asked if he could come to see me about the work I was doing on the speaker. He came to see me at my lab in Crab Orchard, West Virginia, but couldn't stay long because of some other business. While visiting my lab, he said, "I want you to come to San Francisco to talk to my staff about the work you're doing." I said, "That would be great," for in my mind it will justify another trip I want to take on my motorcycle. He called me a few days later and we set a date I could meet his staff in San Francisco, California. We set a date, and he called back to tell me it's not a good idea to ride in Arizona in this June weather. He said, "I'll send you and your daughter Dawn a plane ticket and one for the motorcycle. It'll be in San Francisco, California when you get here." My answer was my motorcycle and trailer were too big to load on an aircraft.

There was one trip I always wanted to take. It would complete most of my plans to ride and to do. That is to ride from El Paso, Texas, over to San Diego, California, up the coast to San Francisco, California, then across the Golden Gate Bridge, and I would have just about done it all.

Our meeting was two weeks from now on a Monday. There was always something that could go wrong.

There was a wedding that my daughter, Dawn, had to go to on the weekend before the meeting. She couldn't get away until Tuesday. So, on Tuesday we took off on my motorcycle ride. We went 640 miles to Memphis the first day. Next day we got to Amarillo, Texas. I've seen this area before, but the next day we got into New Mexico.

P. Allan Hill with his daughter, Dawn Louise Bass, in Texas on a cross-country motorcycle trip.

My daughter, Dawn, loved the sights and so did I, and we saw places I'd never seen before. We spent so much time that I got worried about when would we get to San Francisco. All this day riding was on the back roads, and I got to enjoying it so much I didn't watch the time. We got on Rt. 10 went through Phoenix, and in the middle of June, it was hot. I don't like riding on the big highways like Rt. 10, but I thought I'll take I-10 over to Los Angeles and I'll take the Rt. 1 up the coast to San Francisco. That was a beautiful ride up the coast, but it was Sunday and I've got to be at the meeting on Monday morning. I got to the motel about 10:00 p.m. I don't like to ride in the dark.

The meeting wasn't in San Francisco, California, but in Cupertino, California, just outside San Francisco, California. The next morning Dr. Lemcoe came to the motel to take Dawn and me to breakfast. The meeting was at 9:00 a.m.

I'm just a country boy who plays with projects that's so small most people don't or can't work on. So here I am, the first time in my life in a fancy corporate setting. Dr. Lemcoe, Dawn, and I are on the front side of the table and on the other side were his engineers and business people. The meeting got started. Dr. Lemcoe introduced Dawn and me to his manager in Switzerland. We discussed what I've been working on and what part other companies are doing on other projects. The question came up about the work Dr. Adelman and I had worked on, which was the hearing device for an implant in the ear. Dr. Adelman came into the screen telling the party just what we had done. Dawn and I were introduced to two more company managers.

This was 2009 and I was eighty-one years old. All they wanted to talk about was my motorcycle trip, at that age. Now Dawn told me, we must get back to Crab Orchard, West Virginia, because she has a soccer meeting Saturday and she has to be home by Saturday night.

Dr. Lemcoe hired a chauffeur to take us around after the meeting. I said we must start back home that day, and found out that he booked a hotel for that night and made plans for dinner. Now, I was thinking I had to ride fast to get home on Saturday. We had a whole day seeing a lot of beautiful places. We saw Pebble Beach Golf Course and the area where all the wealthy people go to play golf. He took us to a wonderful place to eat lunch. I didn't know there were redwoods in that part of California. I really didn't feel at ease riding around with a chauffeur. We got to the restaurant at 7:00 p.m. and here comes Dr. Lemcoe with his big car and chauffeur. To me something isn't right when people live like this. Dr. Lemcoe, Dawn, and I went in to eat, and two chauffeurs sat out there just waiting. I'm sure they ate somewhere, but if someone is that rich, can't they spend the money helping the poor? It was a day Dawn and I will remember for the rest of our lives. When someone takes me out to eat, I don't want to splurge, but tonight I ordered lobster and enjoyed it.

I was thinking about the route I would like to take home. Back in 1972, I went to Reno, Nevada, through Rt. I-80, and I would like to see it again. It wasn't hard to get to I-80 from San Francisco. One problem was I really wanted to ride across the Golden Gate Bridge. I had been under the bridge many times while in the US Navy, but I want to go across it again. Dawn explained that it was time to go home, and we'll come back later. I was in such a rush to get to Reno, Nevada, I missed the bridge. That kind of riding isn't fun; but we did get home on Saturday. We took the interstate highways home and bypassed the side roads, which I enjoy so much.

The last trip I took to Key West, Florida, was with my friend Mark Riffe. We didn't even stop at Daytona Beach this time. I have had been to Key West several times. Most times, I went with three or four friends, when we stopped at Daytona first on the way. One trip while in Key West, Gene Deck wanted to get a photo near the famous, "End of Route 1" sign. So we parked our bikes went walking up the street looking for a sign, asking everyone we saw where was the sign. After Gene said his foot was hurting, we decided to give up. We walked back to our bikes and found that we parked under the sign "End of Route 1."

We had been to end of Rt. I North in Maine. We had been "end to end" of a lot of highways. I remember I asked the boys where the end of R-81 South was. On that trip, we had been in Canada since we left Detroit, Michigan. Now we were going to take R-81 from Canada South. I asked where the end is and Gene said, "You've been there a hundred times." It's in Tennessee where Rt. I-81 runs into Rt. I-40 going west. I think I've seen some beautiful sights but the Thousand Islands that you see as you ride from Canada to New York is one of the most beautiful views.

Our bikes have everything you would want: heated seats, heated hand grips, and even radios so we can talk to each other as we ride. We get weather information. We have much better weather gear that we didn't have years before.

My grandson, Robert Allan Morhard, just came back from a trip to California. He is very much like me in that he loves to hike, camp, and travel. He asked me if I wanted to cross the Golden Gate Bridge with him someday. I'm still thinking about a trip across the Golden Gate Bridge…just thinking.

The most exciting trip I had was in Indianapolis, Indiana. I had a strain-gage meeting with Rolls-Royce jet engine company in Indianapolis at noon when we would go to lunch first. I was on my motorcycle as usual when the weather was good. I would get to Indianapolis an hour or so early. So I thought I'll ride west or Rt. I-74 to the next exit and it will be time for me to meet for lunch. I would have gone about ten miles or so and I passed a long truck and when I was near the large wheels of the truck, something happened. A fighter plane was using the truck as a target as if it was going to bomb the truck! As the plane went over the truck, it seemed like it was just a few feet over my head when it opened its after burners and it almost blew my back into the truck. I was so nervous! I couldn't eat an hour later. I think I can stand anything but that one almost got me. At lunch, we discussed the ordeal with the plane and I was told the government had told the pilots to stop using the trucks for a target. If I hadn't been strong and had a big heavy motorcycle, I'm sure the force would have blown me under the truck. I've had many good motorcycle trips but that one was different than most, at least for me.

In 2002, I'd bought a new motorcycle, a top of the line Honda Gold Wing with all the extras, including a matching trailer to tow behind the motorcycle. My daughter, Dawn, had some time to go for a ride. So, I said, "We'll go ride the million-dollar highway in Colorado." On Sunday, we took off. We had planned to get to St. Louis the first day. The weather got wet near Evansville, Indiana. We stopped to put on our rain gear. As I got back on the bike, which was in low gear now, the wind blew me off the bike and I hit my elbow on the gear shift. The motorcycle took off with Dawn on it and the motorcycle went across Rt. I-64 to the other side when she fell off. The trailer hit her in the back. She was lying in some tall weeds beside the road. I went to help her, but she said maybe I broke my back. It was really raining hard. I went to cover her up and I can't find the motorcycle. I followed the path it had made until I saw where it had run into a bank and stopped. I uncovered up the trailer and got some blankets to cover Dawn. By the time I got to her, which only seemed less than five minutes, the ambulance was already there. Someone who saw everything happen called 911, and I was I glad. We went to a hospital. Dawn needed some stitches where her glasses had cut her head. She spent the night in the hospital, and thankfully her back was OK. We rented a car and drove to Louisville, where Mike, Dawn's husband, came to meet us. I went to the Honda shop to tell them to go pick up the bike. I thought it was totaled, although I didn't see it when I went to get the blankets from the trailer. Looking at the bike wasn't on my mind. My friend, Jim Lucas, the Honda dealer, said, "I have a friend who has a truck where he takes a load to Evansville and comes back empty. I'll have him pick up the motorcycle and trailer and it'll save some money." So, the next day Jim called to say the truck driver couldn't pick my bike up. To me the motorcycle had to be totaled, and of course with Dawn injured, I just wasn't thinking and I didn't look at it. The only damage to the bike was a broken mirror, and one scratch on one saddle bag. I had the bike converted to a trike soon after that. The tongue to the trailer was a little twisted and had to be replaced. Other than that, it was just one bad ride.

Most of my short rides have been business related. One that I always found interesting was when traveling to GE Jet Engine Company in Lynn, Massachusetts, to work with their engineers on a new strain gage that I needed to produce. Dawn and I went to Lynn, Massachusetts, to talk to GE engineers about this special gage. I thought I knew what engineering needed, but since GE was paying for the trip, why not take Dawn for a ride? I parked the bike across the street from GE. It was lunch time. I didn't want to go through the extensive process of signing in to the plant. So I met the engineers at a lunch table on the lawn to look at their drawings. I thought, "No problem. I'll have it ready in a week. I had to make some changes on a machine, but nothing too hard to do." This could have been taken care of by fax, but since GE was paying for the information I took advantage of another excuse to ride my motorcycle.

I made many trips to Hi Tech Corp., Pratt & Whitney Jet Engine Division in Hartford, Connecticut, and Pratt & Whitney Jet Engine Division in West Palm Beach, Florida. I made many trips to General Motors–Allison Engine Company before it was sold to Rolls-Royce Company, which was in Indianapolis, Indiana.

I belonged to the Society for Experimental Mechanics (SEM) and attended a conference every year in a different city. Since everyone in the SEM uses strain gages, I tried to attend each SEM conference. When I traveled to the SEM conferences, I'd ride my motorcycle, and I'd wear my leathers. That was what my friends expected to see. One trip was up to Pittsburgh Airport. At the motel, I asked the clerk at the desk if I could park my bike just outside the motel door where it would stay dry overnight. The manager came out to see me. After seeing how beautiful my bike was, he opened the large motor doors and ask me to bring the bike inside the motel for display. Everyone at the meeting knew the motorcycle belonged to whom.

One night around 9:00 p.m. we my best motorcycle friends were visiting me at my home. The moon was bright and the temperature was 75 degrees. So someone said, "Wouldn't this be a good time to ride tonight?" We packed up and took off to Virginia Beach. The weather the next day, Saturday, was expected to be hot, real hot. So, we started out, got to Richmond, and decided to get a room for the night. Gene said, "Let's get up early in the morning and get to the beach before it gets too hot." Gene suggested we call the office to get a wake-up call early in the morning. I said, "Don't worry I get up at 6:00 a.m. every day." Gene woke up at 10:00 a.m. We got to the beach when it was too hot to enjoy the ride.

Denis Riffe is someone who wants to help everyone along the way. On one ride with Denis, Gene, John Morgan, and I were going down a back road in Georgia, and there was a car parked beside the road with a young girl too scared to talk. It took a lot of talking just to get her to pass a note with her mother's phone number so we could call for help. It didn't help much as she saw John Morgan with a long beard. Anyway, Gene and Denis went to call her mother. She still didn't talk to us. I told her I had two young daughters, and I'd look after her.

John and I got in front of the car so she could keep an eye on us and we would guard her. Her mother came to see her. Maybe she wasn't far from the car. Someone in that area had caused trouble, and the girl knew about it. I'm glad we helped the little girl. She sure was glad to see her mother.

About that same summer, I was coming back from Boston. I was on Rt. I-84 in New York behind a large trailer truck. He slowed down and I shot around him. Looking at many state police cars giving tickets to speeders, I usually have my radio on so I can hear the truckers talking to each other, but today I was enjoying my music. The reason the trucks slowed down was we just came into a fifty-five miles per hour sign. I didn't see the sign as I passed the truck, but I did see the police. I thought maybe they can't catch the speed of a motorcycle. I went past the police not sure if I was in trouble or not. I saw an exit not far away. I got off there just in case. Anyway, as I got to the exit, I saw two policemen standing there directing me to where to park. There must have been a dozen cars beside the road. I got a speeding ticket for going seventy-two miles per hour in a fifty-five mile per hour zone. It cost me $135. I explained to the police why I did speed up to get around the truck, but it didn't help. I must say he was as nice as he could have been. I told Gene I got my first speeding ticket on a bike, Gene said, "Would you believe? I got one the same day while going down through Georgia on a back road. I was going seventy-two miles per hour in a fifty-five mile per hour zone." Gene's insurance went up for three years, but thankfully mine didn't. The reason was Gene was on a state road and I was on an interstate highway.

In another ride for three or four days, I rode with Gene Deck, Denis Riffe, Mark Riffe, Robert Skiles, and Robert Deck. Gene made a hotel reservation at the Sea Hawk Inn at Morehead City, North Carolina. We get lined up at the Crab Orchard Baptist Church. Robert Deck, a long-distance truck driver, said, "Let's not go down Rt. 77 to where you pick up Rt. 52. I just came up that way a day ago and the traffic is bad from new roads being built." Gene said, "Will you know more about roads than any of us so lead us to the coast." Robert started out going Rt. 64 east for 150 miles when we need to be going southeast. We got to Clifton Forge, Virginia, on Rt. 220, which goes south all the way to Rt. 40 and maybe that is the best way to go, but as we started I wasn't sure. When we got to Rt. 40, it rained like you have never seen. It flooded the highway. We called the motel to say maybe we can't make it until after midnight. The hotel wanted us to arrive before midnight or they won't be open. We got there at 11:40 p.m. We came home starting up the coast all the way up to Kill Devil Hills, North Carolina. We took many ferries up the coast. Sure, it was a wonderful ride in wonderful weather.

I will always enjoy a motorcycle ride in the warm fresh air as much as ever. You can see so much more of the beautiful land on a motorcycle than you can in a car.

I sure hope the summer this year will bring good motorcycle weather.

I'm now eighty-eight, and last January I was blessed with a nice day here in West Virginia. The temperature was fifty degrees and I went for a one-hundred-mile ride.

My Family History

NEAR THE TURN of the century in 1800, there was a very famous man in Floyd County, Virginia, by the name of Patrick Billy Canaday. He was very well known because he had twenty-one children. One of the children by the name of J. Burl Canaday was the great grandfather of my wife "Hutchie" Lila Lee Horton Hill.

Patrick Billy had two daughters, one named Delila and another Martha. The girls married two boys, who were twins, James and John Morain. James married Martha, and John married Delila. Martha had a daughter and named her Delila after her sister. Delila's daughter married J. R. Hill. Martha, the daughter, married Mr. Commer. Delila died and Mr. Commer died, and J. R. Hill married Martha. The first child born from that marriage was Peter Hill, my grandfather. Out of the marriage of Peter Hill and Jessie Broylis from Princeton, Virginia, were eleven children.

My father, Joseph Alexander Hill ("Zan"), was third from the youngest. Grandpa Hill died at the age of seventy-four in the year 1941. He moved from his farm to the town of Princeton, West Virginia. I heard them say, "He just couldn't take the city life, and he missed the farm."

Grandma always told me I was special and made big sugar cookies and said she made them just for me. Grandma and Grandpa Hill lived on a nice big farm just outside of Princeton, West Virginia, called Hall's Ridge Road. They lived at the end of Hall's Ridge Road. Grandpa Hill was in my opinion a "high-class farmer" and had everything. I guess my recollection was that they were different. They had a big home. One room in the home was a special sitting room with an organ and you only went in there on Sunday or when special company like the preacher came to visit. They had buildings like one for making cheese, and one where Grandpa kept his tobacco drying on a loft. There was a big farm barn for everything you could use.

Dad had ten brothers and sisters, so you can see I had a lot of cousins. I thought I was Grandma's favorite grandchild because she made these big cookies and told me they were for me. I guess my ancestors were just about the longest living around. Dad was ninety-six and choked to death. Grandma asked me to come see her because she was sick. I lived in Philadelphia,

Pennsylvania, but I went to Princeton, West Virginia, one weekend to see her. To my surprise, she wasn't worried about herself because she was looking after her son next door. He was eighty-six years old. Grandma was 107 years old. She had never been in a hospital and spent less than one hundred dollars in her life on medical bills. She died at the age of 107.

I didn't know much about the Hill's side of the family. When Grandpa died, Dad and I went to Princeton, West Virginia. Dad's youngest brothers did not go to the funeral. I was about ten years old then and Dad told me they were in jail because they shot a "moonshiner." I didn't think any more about it. Just before Dad died, I saw a girl who was a Hill, and I asked her about the "moon-shine" story. She said her dad was Earl Hill. Now I know some one knew the history of my uncle Earl. I wanted to know the history about her Granddad, and she told me the shocking news. My uncle Posie and Earl had a fight on Saturday night while drinking. A man beat them up, so Sunday morning my uncle Posie and Earl found the boy who beat them up. They had a sawmill in Princeton, West Virginia, and they took the boy to the sawmill and cut his head off. Dad said the story is true. I didn't want to know any more about the Hill side of the family.

The Browning side of the family is harder to describe. My grandfather was a saw sharpener for the Rotter Lumber Co. at Mabin, West Virginia. He was in his early forties when he died from the metal filings that sharpened the saws. Grandma Ball was his second marriage. In the first marriage they had four children. When his first wife died, he married Grandma. She was from Tug river, the same place where the Hatfields and McCoys lived and fought their famous feud.

My grandma and Mr. Browning mother's father had four children, my mother being the old-est. She had to take care of the baby from the first family. Mother's name was Hattie. Next was Aunt Mary, Aunt Ruth, and Uncle Evert. Uncle Evert was killed in the mine at Bud when he was about twenty years old.

When my grandfather, whom I never knew, died, Grandma married Wesley Ball, and they had three girls. Since mother was in the middle bunch, I always thought of the ones on the end as my uncles and aunts. The family was close and one big family. Grandma was a very hard worker. I knew all about the Ball family because when Dad and mother had their troubles, I was sent to visit Grandma Ball, which was not too far away. I could ride a train for ten dollars from Bud, West Virginia, to Mabin, West Virginia. When I got off the train in Mabin, I had to walk approximately five miles to where Grandma lived.

Grandma 's house was about two miles from any other home. The home was a small log home, with a large fireplace. At night, they would gather around the fireplace and tell stories. To me it must have been cold all the time, because all I remember was sitting around the fireplace. They had a small room added to the log home for the kitchen where they ate and cooked. Things were bad. They didn't have any money, and even the lamp oil was scarce so they extinguished the light as soon as the dishes were put away. The room downstairs was just one small room with the fireplace. That was where they slept and visited. There was an upstairs; but you had to go outside to go to the beds up there. The beds had a down mattress, which was about eighteen inches thick. You haven't enjoyed a good night's sleep until you slept in a mattress made of goose feathers. I remember being out in the yard with Grandma making hominy in a large black stew pot over a fire when I heard an odd noise. I looked up and saw my first airplane. Grandma's family was about the poorest people I knew, but I don't guess anyone ever went to bed hungry. No radios, no phones.

The next farm over the hill approximately two miles had young boys, as most country people they had moonshine and a party. As far as I know there wasn't any moonshine at Grandma's home. I don't know where the boys went to have a party, but they did and at night as they would walk home going by Grandma's home. The boys would come through the bedroom to get a drink of water on the way home. As for the parties, I remember one weekend when Grandma removed everything from the one small room and had a dance party at her log home. There were three girls of hers and three or four boys from across the hill.

Grandma was self-supporting. She had sheep, which supplied meat as well as wool. That was exciting helping shear the sheep. I always felt sorry for them after they lost their coats. I liked sheep, but I hated the geese because they chased me with a hiss and I'm sure they would have bitten me if they could have caught me. Grandma made her soap and of course canned everything. Honey was a part of everyday food on the table. She liked her bees and she could rob the beehive with no fear of being stung. She said, "They know if you're afraid and will sting you." She loved them and her sheep. You wouldn't say Grandma was a farmer, but she just did what was necessary to survive. The boys across the hill were hunters and had dogs for each hunting trip. Coonhounds, rabbit dogs, and squirrel dogs. The dogs liked to chase sheep. Sometimes they would wander over to Grandma's and kill a sheep. Grandma would get her shotgun out and now there was a dead dog. She was known never to waste a shell. When she shot at something, she didn't miss anything she shot at. This can cause problems with neighbors.

This is a story a school teacher asked me a few years ago. The neighbor's names were Burchfield, and this teacher asked me if the story was true. So I researched it and this was what I found. The Burchfield boys had a special dog that came over to the sheep farm. Grandma didn't want to kill the dog and she just wanted to keep it away from her sheep. I don't know how Grandma caught the dog but she did. She got a corn knob, put something on it, and rubbed up the rectum of the dog and it went crazy and ran home. The father of the son to whom the dog belonged thought the dog was mad. Now the only way to take care of a mad dog was to kill it. So the dog was killed. Now as families are, there were girls at the Ball home and boys at the Burchfield home, and they got together sometimes. One of the Ball girls told one of the Burchfield girls about what Grandma had done to one of the dogs. It wasn't long before the boy got the news. His dog wasn't mad after all and it shouldn't be dead. Now Grandma was in trouble. I don't know where on the creek or on bridge, but the boy, Victor Birchfield, saw Grandma on the bridge and he pushed her into the creek. The boy went to jail, but they let him go to the Civilian Conservation Corps after the jail time. Victor went to fight in World War II. Victor is now a very well-known police officer. I went to Victor and asked his side of the story. He confirmed that was the way it happened. I spent a lot of time at Grandma's, but it was the early years I remembered best. It wasn't a visit, but it was to get me away from all the troubles at home.

Things never got better—I guess I learned to live with it.

Looking back on all the family problems, it was clear that my Dad was a crazy man, but also a genius in many ways. He could do so many things, and master all of them. I've seen him stand on the end of a telephone pole waiting for another piece of telephone pole to be passed to him, so he could secure the two poles together.

My brother, David, is ten and a half years younger than I am and is the owner of David Hill Cement Co. David and I talk about Dad and say Dad taught us things you don't read in a book. David didn't see some of the things I lived through.

There were seven of us children. I'm the oldest.

- Sister—Rosalyn, a year and a half younger than me; died of cancer in 2011
- Brother—Garman, four and a half years younger; died of alcoholism in 2002
- Brother—David, ten and a half years younger
- Brother—Peter, thirteen years younger; died in 2003. He was never married and was a loner
- Sister—Lou, fifteen years younger; died of cancer in 2005
- Sister—Sue, eighteen years younger; died of cancer in 2010

I have two daughters: Jane Morhard and Dawn Bass. Jane lives in Southport, North Carolina, with her husband Bob, and they have three children: Lauren, Ryan, and Robert. Ryan is married to Young, and they have one child, Allan. Dawn lives in West Virginia and was married to Mike, who unfortunately is deceased, and they have two children, Erin and Anne.

P. Allan Hill and his family in Crab Orchard, West Virginia (2016).

Jane and Bob Morhard with their family (2016).

Mike and Dawn Bass with their family (2000).